THE
INNOVATOR'S
COOKBOOK

Also by Steven Johnson

Interface Culture: How New Technology Transforms
the Way We Create and Communicate

Emergence: The Connected Lives of Ants,
Brains, Cities, and Software

Mind Wide Open: Your Brain and the Neuroscience of Everyday Life

Everything Bad Is Good for You: How Today's Popular Culture
Is Actually Making Us Smarter

The Ghost Map: The Story of London's Most Terrifying Epidemic—
and How It Changed Science, Cities, and the Modern World

The Invention of Air: A Story of Science, Faith, Revolution,
and the Birth of America

Where Good Ideas Come From

THE INNOVATOR'S COOKBOOK

ESSENTIALS
FOR
INVENTING
WHAT IS NEXT

EDITED BY

Steven Johnson

RIVERHEAD BOOKS
NEW YORK

RIVERHEAD BOOKS
Published by the Penguin Group
Penguin Group (USA) Inc.
375 Hudson Street, New York, New York 10014, USA
Penguin Group (Canada), 90 Eglinton Avenue East, Suite 700, Toronto,
Ontario M4P 2Y3, Canada (a division of Pearson Penguin Canada Inc.)
Penguin Books Ltd., 80 Strand, London WC2R 0RL, England
Penguin Group Ireland, 25 St. Stephen's Green, Dublin 2, Ireland
(a division of Penguin Books Ltd.)
Penguin Group (Australia), 250 Camberwell Road, Camberwell, Victoria 3124,
Australia (a division of Pearson Australia Group Pty. Ltd.)
Penguin Books India Pvt. Ltd., 11 Community Centre, Panchsheel Park,
New Delhi—110 017, India
Penguin Group (NZ), 67 Apollo Drive, Rosedale, Auckland 0632, New Zealand
(a division of Pearson New Zealand Ltd.)
Penguin Books (South Africa) (Pty.) Ltd., 24 Sturdee Avenue, Rosebank,
Johannesburg 2196, South Africa

Penguin Books Ltd., Registered Offices: 80 Strand, London WC2R 0RL, England

While the author has made every effort to provide accurate telephone numbers and
Internet addresses at the time of publication, neither the publisher nor the author assumes
any responsibility for errors, or for changes that occur after publication. Further, the
publisher does not have any control over and does not assume any responsibility for author
or third-party websites or their content.

THE INNOVATOR'S COOKBOOK

First Riverhead trade paperback edition: October 2011
Riverhead trade paperback ISBN: 978-1-59448-558-9

PRINTED IN THE UNITED STATES OF AMERICA

10 9 8 7 6 5 4 3 2 1

CONTENTS

INNOVATORS AT WORK

INTRODUCTION

The first step in winning the future is encouraging
American innovation.
— BARACK OBAMA, STATE OF THE UNION ADDRESS,
JANUARY 2011

I first began working explicitly on the problem of innovation in the summer of 2006, when I started writing a book about new ideas and the environments that encouraged them. But it wasn't until I finished that book that I realized I had been wrestling with innovation, in one way or another, for almost two decades. The first articles I published in my twenties as an easily distracted English-lit grad student gravitated toward the digital revolutions coming out of Silicon Valley; all my books since then have focused on new ideas and their transformative power—innovations in science or tech or politics or entertainment, some of them recent headlines and some ancient history.

That long history with the topic may help explain why I assumed almost by default, as I was writing the innovation book, that there was nothing particularly *timely* about the subject matter, nothing distinct to the zeitgeist of postmillennial culture.

Sure, we routinely lavish praise on and pen hagiographies about entrepreneurs like Steve Jobs and Mark Zuckerberg, but we did the same for Thomas Edison and Ben Franklin before them. I had written books that I consciously thought of as zeitgeist-y as I was working on them. Innovation wasn't like that. This was, in fact, one of the things I found refreshing about the topic. Innovation wasn't trendy; it was evergreen.

But then something seemed to happen, as the world economy began to climb its way out of the Great Crunch of 2008 to 2009, and we began to probe through the rubble looking for clues to explain what had brought on such a colossal failure, clues that might also, we hoped, suggest ways to avoid similar failures in the future. After a decade of financial pseudo innovation—the credit-default swaps and collateralized debt obligations that inflated the housing bubble and nearly brought down the world economy when that bubble inevitably burst—it seemed suddenly, viscerally clear that economic growth needed to come from making *useful things* again, whether those things were electric cars or digital code, and not just creating illusory value out of complex derivative schemes.

I saw this firsthand in the United States, and to a lesser extent in the UK, but I suspect the pattern extends throughout the world. By the time I had finished the final draft of my book, innovation seemed to be on everyone's lips: public school superintendents, venture capitalists, clean-energy entrepreneurs, op-ed writers. And so when President Obama delivered his State of the Union address in January of 2011, it was not terribly surprising to see him devote nearly a third of the speech to innovation-related initiatives. The speech is worth quoting from in some length, because the way that he frames the issue tells us something important about why innovation seems so central to us today:

> The first step in winning the future is encouraging American innovation. None of us can predict with certainty what the next big industry will be or where the new jobs will come from. Thirty years ago, we couldn't know that something called the Internet would lead to an economic revolution. What we can do—what America does better than anyone else—is spark the creativity and imagination of our people. We're the nation that put cars in driveways and computers in offices; the nation of Edison and the Wright brothers; of Google and Facebook. In America, innovation doesn't just change our lives. It is how we make our living.
>
> Our free-enterprise system is what drives innovation. But because it's not always profitable for companies to invest in basic research, throughout our history, our government has provided cutting-edge scientists and inventors with the support that they need. That's what planted the seeds for the Internet. That's what helped make possible things like computer chips and GPS. Just think of all the good jobs—from manufacturing to retail—that have come from these breakthroughs.
>
> Half a century ago, when the Soviets beat us into space with the launch of a satellite called Sputnik, we had no idea how we would beat them to the moon. The science wasn't even there yet. NASA didn't exist. But after investing in better research and education, we didn't just surpass the Soviets; we unleashed a wave of innovation that created new industries and millions of new jobs.

This is our generation's Sputnik moment. Two years ago, I said that we needed to reach a level of research and development we haven't seen since the height of the Space Race. And in a few weeks, I will be sending a budget to Congress that helps us meet that goal. We'll invest in biomedical research, information technology, and especially clean energy technology—an investment that will strengthen our security, protect our planet, and create countless new jobs for our people.

As Obama suggests, the social impact of innovation has a long history to it, one that, it should be said, is hardly as America-centric as Obama implies: think of the British steam engines that powered the first wave of the industrial revolution in the eighteenth century, or the inventions in algebra and double-entry accounting during the Islamic golden age more than a thousand years ago. The history of human progress, worldwide, is the history of new ideas put to wonderful new use.

But the State of the Union address also shed light on what makes our present attitude toward innovation different, in two fundamental ways. The first is this distinct assumption that innovation can—and should—be *cultivated;* that it wasn't just something that would magically emerge on its own from the folkloric Entrepreneurial American Spirit. Innovation could be taught, encouraged, supported—or suppressed—thanks to decisions that we made as a society. It wasn't enough just to lower the capital gains tax and let the entrepreneurs and venture capitalists go wild; innovation required more subtle interventions for it to truly flourish.

The president's interest in nurturing innovation has its roots in a growing body of research that has accumulated over the past

twenty years, some of it written by economists and legal scholars who would become part of Obama's inner circle. For most of
the twentieth century, innovation lived at the margins of most
economics scholarship. Thousands of books were written on the
efficiency of markets, and the conditions under which governments might correct capitalism's turbulence or inequities; elabo-
rate mathematical models were built to explain the miracles of
price signaling. But the seemingly equally important question of
how societies came up with new products in the first place went
largely unexamined. Intriguingly, some of the most astute analyses of innovation came from open critics of capitalism: starting
with Marx's famous observation that market-driven economies
created a culture of permanent change, where "all that is solid
melts into air." Later, the Austrian socialist Joseph Schumpeter
chronicled capitalism's relentless drive for "creative destruction"—
popularizing a phrase that would eventually be embraced by titans of industry and business school seminars, losing its original
negative connotations in the process.

But the past two decades have corrected this strange oversight,
as a growing number of influential thinkers have begun to investigate the mysteries of innovation, many of whom are represented
in this volume. Books with titles like *The Innovator's Dilemma* and
The Art of Innovation now circulate through business school syl-
labi and corporate retreats. Creativity consultants do a booming
business. Cities around the globe vie to re-create the innovation
magic of high-tech hubs like Silicon Valley or Route 128.

The Innovator's Cookbook is, in part, an attempt to capture the
best of that wide-ranging scholarship in a single volume. But it
is also an attempt to shine light on a more recent development in
the literature of innovation, one that is also evident in Obama's

State of the Union address. And that is the growing sense that governments have an integral role to play in fostering innovative societies—and, perhaps more radically, that they themselves can show some of the inventiveness that has traditionally been the hallmark of the private sector. While the scholarship on innovation that has blossomed over the past twenty years has opened many doors in understanding how new products and services emerge, it has generally worked under the assumption that the most important innovations arose out of the competitive pressure of the marketplace. But the revolutionary impact of the Internet and the Web—the two most transformative innovations of our time, both of which evolved outside traditional market environments and are, effectively, owned and operated collectively—have made it clear that the private sector hardly holds a monopoly on innovation.

I suspect the most important breakthroughs over the next ten years will come from hybrid environments, where the public and private sectors overlap. Consider two examples from the past few years: Kickstarter and SeeClickFix. Kickstarter is a site that allows individuals to fund creative projects, like movies, art installations, albums, and so on. Donors may get special gifts in return for their contributions—signed copies of the final CD or an invitation to the opening—but they do not own the creations they help support. In just two years of existence, Kickstarter has raised more than $60 million for thousands of projects, taking a small cut of each transaction. The economic exchange that Kickstarter enables between donors and creators works outside the traditional logic of markets. People are "investing" in others not for the promise of subsequent financial reward, but rather for the social rewards of supporting important work. The artists, on the other hand, are relying on a decentralized network of support, not government grants. And yet Kickstarter itself is a for-profit company that may well make a nice return for its own investors and founders.

SeeClickFix is a mobile app that allows community members to report open fire hydrants, dangerous intersections, threatening tree limbs, and other pressing local needs. (A related service, FixMyStreet, launched in the UK several years ago.) In proper Web 2.0 fashion, all complaints are visible to the community, and other members can vote to endorse the problem. SeeClickFix has begun offering free dashboards for local governments, with a premium service available for a monthly fee. The service also bundles together its user-generated reports and e-mails them to the appropriate authorities in each market. It's an intriguing hybrid model: the private sector creates the interfaces for managing and mapping urban issues, while the public sector continues its traditional role of resolving those issues.

What I love about these services is not just the laudable goals they both set out to accomplish, but the inventiveness of the approaches they take. They are each tackling a long-standing social problem: How do we support artists whose work is not yet sustained by the marketplace? How do we monitor all the changing needs of real-world neighborhoods? But their methods are amazingly novel—so novel, in fact, that you might be inclined to suspect that they might never work in practice. But the same skepticism was said of a user-authored encyclopedia that Jimmy Wales launched ten years ago—and now Wikipedia regularly outperforms the *Encyclopedia Britannica*. That these unlikely projects actually turn out to work in practice is a testament not only to the new technologies of the Web and mobile computing; it's also a testament to the adventurousness of the general public, the people who actually use and support these services, and in many cases expand their range—a process that Columbia's Amar Bhidé calls "venturesome consumption."

This is the great opportunity of our time: we have both extraordinary new tools that allow us to build things like Kickstarter and SeeClickFix *and* we have a society of consumers and citizens who are willing to experiment with these crazy new schemes, so much so that what seemed crazy two years ago now just seems routine. The ideas assembled in this book—particularly in the conversations with "innovators at work" in the second half—are all, in their different ways, wrestling with the question of how best to capitalize on that opportunity. New ideas have been driving human progress since the Stone Age; what we have now is a growing set of new ideas about how to generate new ideas. Many of those ideas will come out of private-sector start-ups, but just as many will come from outside the marketplace: from universities, and nonprofits, and, yes, even governments. In this sense, *The Innovator's Cookbook* is not unlike what you find in the traditional variety of cookbooks: the best recipes draw their flavors from multiple cuisines. The Internet has been the most powerful driver of innovation in our time in large part because it drew upon ideas from university scholarship, military research, visionary start-ups, open-source collaborations—not to mention all those venturesome consumers figuring out amazing new uses for the technology. The ideas that will "win the future"—in the United States, and everywhere else—will no doubt be concocted out of equally diverse ingredients.

Steven Johnson
May 2011

ESSAYS

The Discipline of Innovation

PETER DRUCKER

Despite much discussion these days of the "entrepreneurial personality," few of the entrepreneurs with whom I have worked during the past thirty years had such personalities. But I have known many people—say salespeople, surgeons, journalists, scholars, even musicians—who did have them without being the least bit entrepreneurial. What all the successful entrepreneurs I have met have in common is not a certain kind of personality but a commitment to the systematic practice of innovation.

Innovation is the specific function of entrepreneurship, whether in an existing business, a public service institution, or a new venture started by a lone individual in the family kitchen. It is the means by which the entrepreneur either creates new wealth-producing resources or endows existing resources with enhanced potential for creating wealth.

Today, much confusion exists about the proper definition of

entrepreneurship. Some observers use the term to refer to all small businesses; others, to all new businesses. In practice, however, a great many well-established businesses engage in highly successful entrepreneurship. The term, then, refers not to an enterprise's size or age but to a certain kind of activity. At the heart of that activity is innovation: the effort to create purposeful, focused change in an enterprise's economic or social potential.

SOURCES OF INNOVATION

There are, of course, innovations that spring from a flash of genius. Most innovations, however, especially the successful ones, result from a conscious, purposeful search for innovation opportunities, which are found only in a few situations. Four such areas of opportunity exist within a company or industry: unexpected occurrences, incongruities, process needs, and industry and market changes.

Three additional sources of opportunity exist outside a company in its social and intellectual environment: demographic change, changes in perception, and new knowledge.

True, these sources overlap, different as they may be in the nature of their risk, difficulty, and complexity, and the potential for innovation may well lie in more than one area at a time. But together, they account for the great majority of all innovation opportunities.

1. Unexpected Occurrences

Consider, first, the easiest and simplest source of innovation opportunity: the unexpected. In the early 1930s, IBM developed the first modern accounting machine, which was designed for banks. But banks in 1933 did not buy new equipment. What saved the company—according to a story that Thomas Watson Sr., the company's founder and long-term CEO, often told—was its exploitation of an unexpected success: The New York Public Library wanted to buy a machine. Unlike the banks, libraries in those early New Deal days had money, and Watson sold more than a hundred of his otherwise unsalable machines to libraries.

Fifteen years later, when everyone believed that computers were designed for advanced scientific work, business unexpectedly showed an interest in a machine that could do payroll. Univac, which had the most advanced machine, spurned business applications. But IBM immediately realized it faced a possible unexpected success, redesigned what was basically Univac's machine for such mundane applications as payroll, and within five years became a leader in the computer industry, a position it has maintained to this day.

The unexpected failure may be an equally important source of innovation opportunities. Everyone knows about the Ford Edsel as the biggest new-car failure in automotive history. What very few people seem to know, however, is that the Edsel's failure was the foundation for much of the company's later success. Ford planned the Edsel, the most carefully designed car to that point in American automotive history, to give the company a full product line with which to compete with General Motors. When it bombed, despite all the planning, market research, and design that had gone into it, Ford realized that something was happening in the automobile market that ran counter to the basic assumptions on which GM and everyone else had been designing and marketing cars. No longer was the market segmented primarily by income groups; the new principle of segmentation was what we now call "lifestyles." Ford's response was the Mustang, a car that gave the company a distinct personality and reestablished it as an industry leader.

Unexpected successes and failures are such productive sources of innovation opportunities because most businesses dismiss them, disregard them, and even resent them. The German scientist who around 1905 synthesized novocaine, the first nonaddictive narcotic, had intended it to be used in major surgical procedures like amputations. Surgeons, however, preferred total anesthesia for such procedures; they still do. Instead, novocaine found a ready appeal among dentists. Its inventor spent the remaining years of his life traveling from dental school to dental school making speeches that forbade dentists from "misusing" his noble invention in applications for which he had not intended it.

This is a caricature, to be sure, but it illustrates the attitude managers often take to the unexpected: "It should not have happened." Corporate reporting systems further ingrain this reaction, for they draw attention away from unanticipated possibilities. The typical monthly or quarterly report has on its first page a list of problems—that is, the areas where results fall short of expectations. Such information is needed, of course, to help prevent deterioration of performance. But it also suppresses the recognition of new opportunities. The first acknowledgment of a possible opportunity usually applies to an area in which a company does better than budgeted. Thus genuinely entrepreneurial businesses have two "first pages"—a problem page and an opportunity page—and managers spend equal time on both.

2. Incongruities

Alcon Laboratories was one of the success stories of the 1960s because Bill Conner, the company's cofounder, exploited an incongruity in medical technology. The cataract operation is the world's third or fourth most common surgical procedure. During the past three hundred years, doctors systematized it to the point that the only "old-fashioned" step left was the cutting of a ligament. Eye surgeons had learned to cut the ligament with complete success, but it was so different a procedure from the rest of the operation, and so incompatible with it, that they often dreaded it. It was incongruous.

Doctors had known for fifty years about an enzyme that could dissolve the ligament without cutting. All Conner did was to add a preservative to this enzyme that gave it a few months' shelf life. Eye surgeons immediately accepted the new compound, and Alcon found itself with a worldwide monopoly. Fifteen years later, Nestlé bought the company for a fancy price.

Such an incongruity within the logic or rhythm of a process is only one possibility out of which innovation opportunities may arise. Another source is incongruity between economic realities. For instance, whenever an industry has a steadily growing market but falling profit margins—as say, in the steel industries of developed countries between 1950 and 1970—an incongruity exists. The innovative response: minimills.

An incongruity between expectations and results can also open up possibilities for innovation. For fifty years after the turn of the century, shipbuilders and shipping companies worked hard both to make ships faster and to lower their fuel consumption. Even so, the more successful they were in boosting speed and trimming their fuel needs, the worse the economics of ocean freighters became. By 1950 or so, the ocean freighter was dying, if not already dead.

All that was wrong, however, was an incongruity between the industry's assumptions and its realities. The real costs did not come from doing work (that is, being at sea) but from *not* doing work (that is, sitting idle in port). Once managers understood where costs truly lay, the innovations were obvious: the roll-on and roll-off ship and the container ship. These solutions, which involved old technology, simply applied to the ocean freighters what railroads and truckers had been using for thirty years. A shift in viewpoint, not in technology, totally changed the economics of ocean shipping and turned it into one of the major growth industries of the last twenty to thirty years.

3. Process Needs

Anyone who has ever driven in Japan knows that the country has no modern highway system. Its roads still follow the paths laid down for—or by—oxcarts in the tenth century. What makes the system work for automobiles and trucks is an adaptation of the reflector used on American highways since the early 1930s. The reflector lets each car see which other cars are approaching from any one of a half-dozen directions. This minor invention, which enables traffic to move smoothly and with a minimum of accidents, exploited a process need.

What we now call the media had its origin in two innovations developed around 1890 in response to process needs. One was Ottmar Mergenthaler's Linotype, which made it possible to produce newspapers quickly and in large volume. The other was a social innovation, modern advertising, invented by the first true newspaper publishers, Adolph Ochs of the *New York Times*, Joseph Pulitzer of the *New York World*, and William Randolph Hearst. Advertising made it possible for them to distribute news practically free of charge, with the profit coming from marketing.

4. Industry and Market Changes

Managers may believe that industry structures are ordained by the good Lord, but these structures can—and often do—change overnight. Such change creates tremendous opportunity for innovation.

One of American business's great success stories in recent decades is the brokerage firm of Donaldson, Lufkin & Jenrette, recently acquired by the Equitable Life Assurance Society. DL&J was founded in 1960 by three young men, all graduates of the Harvard Business School, who realized that the structure of the financial industry was changing as institutional investors became dominant. These young men had practically no capital and no connections. Still, within a few years, their firm had become a leader in the move to negotiated commissions and one of Wall Street's stellar performers. It was the first to be incorporated and go public.

In a similar fashion, changes in industry structure have created massive innovation opportunities for American health care providers. During the past ten or fifteen years, independent surgical and psychiatric clinics, emergency centers, and HMOs have opened throughout the country. Comparable opportunities in telecommunications followed industry upheavals—in transmission (with the emergence of MCI and Sprint in long-distance service) and in equipment (with the emergence of such companies as Rolm in the manufacturing of private branch exchanges).

When an industry grows quickly—the critical figure seems to be in the neighborhood of 40 percent growth in ten years or less—its structure changes. Established companies, concentrating on defending what they already have, tend not to counterattack when a newcomer challenges them. Indeed, when market or industry structures change, traditional industry leaders again and again neglect the fastest-growing market segments. New opportunities rarely fit the way the industry has always approached the market, defined it, or organized to serve it. Innovators, therefore, have a good chance of being left alone for a long time.

5. Demographic Changes

Of the outside sources of innovation opportunities, demographics are the most reliable. Demographic events have known lead times; for instance, every person who will be in the American labor force by the year 2000 has already been born. Yet because policymakers often neglect demographics, those who watch them and exploit them can reap great rewards.

The Japanese are ahead in robotics because they paid attention to demographics. Everyone in the developed countries around 1970 or so knew that there was both a baby bust and an education explosion going on; about half or more of the young people were staying in school beyond high school. Consequently, the number of people available for traditional blue-collar work in manufacturing was bound to decrease and become inadequate by 1990. Everyone knew this, but only the Japanese acted on it, and they now have a ten-year lead in robotics.

Much the same is true of Club Mediterranee's success in the travel and resort business. By 1970, thoughtful observers could have seen the emergence of large numbers of affluent and educated young adults in Europe and the United States. Not comfortable with the kind of vacations their working-class parents had enjoyed—the summer weeks at Brighton or Atlantic City—these young people were ideal customers for a new and exotic version of the "hangout" of their teen years.

Managers have known for a long time that demographics matter, but they have always believed that population statistics change slowly. In this century, however, they don't. Indeed, the innovation opportunities made possible by changes in the numbers of people—and in their age distribution, education, occupations, and geographic location—are among the most rewarding and least risky of entrepreneurial pursuits.

6. Changes in Perception

"The glass is half full" and "The glass is half empty" are descriptions of the same phenomenon but have vastly different meanings. Changing a manager's perception of a glass from half full to half empty opens up big innovation opportunities.

All factual evidence indicates, for instance, that in the last twenty years, Americans' health has improved with unprecedented speed—whether measured by mortality rates for the newborn, survival rates for the very old, the incidence of cancers (other than lung cancer), cancer cure rates, or other factors. Even so, collective hypochondria grips the nation. Never before has there been so much concern with or fear about health. Suddenly, everything seems to cause cancer or degenerative heart disease or premature loss of memory. The glass is clearly half empty.

Rather than rejoicing in great improvements in health, Americans seem to be emphasizing how far away they still are from immortality. This view of things has created many opportunities for innovations: markets for new health care magazines, for exercise classes and jogging equipment, and for all kinds of health foods. The fastest-growing new U.S. business in 1983 was a company that makes indoor exercise equipment.

A change in perception does not alter facts. It changes their meaning, though—and very quickly. It took less than two years for the computer to change from being perceived as a threat and as something only big businesses would use to something one buys for doing income tax. Economics do not necessarily dictate such a change; in fact, they may be irrelevant. What determines whether people see a glass as half full or half empty is mood rather than fact, and a change in mood often defies quantification. But it is not exotic. It is concrete. It can be defined. It can be tested. And it can be exploited for innovation opportunity.

7. New Knowledge

Among history-making innovations, those that are based on new knowledge—whether scientific, technical, or social—rank high. They are the superstars of entrepreneurship; they get the publicity and the money. They are what people usually mean when they talk of innovation, although not all innovations based on knowledge are important.

Knowledge-based innovations differ from all others in the time they take, in their casualty rates, and in their predictability, as well as in the challenges they pose to entrepreneurs. Like most superstars, they can be temperamental, capricious, and hard to direct. They have, for instance, the longest lead time of all innovations. There is a protracted span between the emergence of new knowledge and its distillation into usable technology. Then there is another long period before this new technology appears in the marketplace in products, processes, or services. Overall, the lead time involved is something like fifty years, a figure that has not shortened appreciably throughout history.

To become effective, innovation of this sort usually demands not one kind of knowledge but many. Consider one of the most potent knowledge-based innovations: modern banking. The theory of the entrepreneurial bank—that is, of the purposeful use of capital to general economic development—was formulated by the Comte de Saint-Simon during the era of Napoleon. Despite Saint-Simon's extraordinary prominence, it was not until thirty years after his death in 1825 that two of his disciples, the brothers Jacob and Isaac Pereire, established the first entrepreneurial bank, the Credit Mobilier, and ushered in what we now call finance capitalism.

The Pereires, however, did not know modern commercial banking, which developed at about the same time across the channel in England. The Credit Mobilier, failed ignominiously. A few years later, two young men—one an American, J. P. Morgan, and one a German, Georg Siemens—put together the French theory of entrepreneurial banking and the English theory of commercial banking to create the first successful modern banks: J.P. Morgan & Company in New York, and the Deutsche Bank in Berlin. Ten years later, a young Japanese, Shibusawa Eiichi, adapted Siemens's concept to his country and thereby laid the foundation of Japan's modern economy. This is how knowledge-based innovation always works.

The computer, to cite another example, required no fewer than six separate strands of knowledge:

- binary arithmetic
- Charles Babbage's conception of a calculating machine, in the first half of the nineteenth century
- the punch card, invented by Herman Hollerith for the U.S. census of 1890
- the audion tube, an electronic switch invented in 1906
- symbolic logic, which was developed between 1910 and 1913 by Bertrand Russell and Alfred North Whitehead
- concepts of programming and feedback that came out of the abortive attempts during World War I to develop effective antiaircraft guns

Although all the necessary knowledge was available by 1918, the first operational digital computer did not appear until 1946.

Long lead times and the needs for convergence among different kinds of knowledge explain the peculiar rhythm of knowledge-based innovation, its attractions, and its dangers. During a long gestation period, there is a lot of talk and little action. Then, when all the elements suddenly converge, there is tremendous excitement and activity and an enormous amount of speculation. Between 1880 and 1890, for example, almost one thousand electronic-apparatus companies were founded in developed countries. Then, as always, there was a crash and a shakeout. By 1914, only twenty-five were still alive. In the early 1920s, three hundred to five hundred automobile companies existed in the United States; by 1960, only four of them remained.

It may be difficult, but knowledge-based innovation can be managed. Success requires careful analysis of the various kinds of knowledge needed to make an innovation possible. Both J. P. Morgan and Georg Siemens did this when they established their banking ventures. The Wright brothers did this when they developed the first operational airplane.

Careful analysis of the needs—and above all, the capabilities—of the intended user is also essential. It may seem paradoxical, but knowledge-based innovation is more market dependent than any other kind of innovation. De Havilland, a British company, designed and built the first passenger jet, but it did not analyze what the market needed and therefore did not identify two key factors. One was configuration—that is, the right size with the right payload for the routes on which a jet would give an airline the greatest advantage. The other was equally mundane: How could the airlines finance the purchase of such an expensive plane? Because de Havilland failed to do an adequate user analysis, two American companies, Boeing and Douglas, took over the commercial jet-aircraft industry.

PRINCIPLES OF INNOVATION

Purposeful, systematic innovation begins with the analysis of the sources of new opportunities. Depending on the context, sources will have different importance at different times. Demographics, for instance, may be of little concern to innovators of fundamental industrial processes like steelmaking, although the Linotype machine became successful primarily because there were not enough skilled typesetters available to satisfy a mass market. By the same token, new knowledge may be of little relevance to someone innovating a social instrument to satisfy a need that changing demographics or tax laws have created. But whatever the situation, innovators must analyze all opportunity sources.

Because innovation is both conceptual and perceptual, would-be innovators must also go out and look, ask, and listen. Successful innovators use both the right and left sides of their brains. They work out analytically what the innovation has to be to satisfy an opportunity. Then they go out and look at potential users to study their expectations, their values, and their needs.

To be effective, an innovation has to be simple, and it has to be focused. It should do only one thing; otherwise it confuses people. Indeed, the greatest praise an innovation can receive is for people to say, "This is obvious! Why didn't I think of it? It's so simple!" Even the innovation that creates new uses and new markets should be directed toward a specific, clear, and carefully designed application.

Effective innovations start small. They are not grandiose. It may be to enable a moving vehicle to draw electric power while it runs along rails, the innovation that made possible the electric streetcar. Or it may be the elementary idea of putting the same number of matches into a matchbox (it used to be fifty). This simple notion made possible the automatic filling of matchboxes and gave the Swedes a world monopoly on matches for half a century. By contrast, grandiose ideas for things that will "revolution ize an industry" are unlikely to work.

In fact, no one can foretell whether a given innovation will end up a big business or a modest achievement. But even if the results are modest, the successful innovation aims from the beginning to become the standard setter, to determine the direction of a new technology or a new industry, to create the business that is—and remains—ahead of the pack. If an innovation does not aim at leadership from the beginning, it is unlikely to be innovative enough.

Above all, innovation is work rather than genius. It requires knowledge. It often requires ingenuity. And it requires focus. There are clearly people who are more talented innovators than others, but their talents lie in well-defined areas. Indeed, innovators rarely work in more than one area. For all his systematic innovative accomplishments, Thomas Edison worked only in the electrical field. An innovator in financial areas, Citibank, for example, is not likely to embark on innovations in health care.

In innovation, as in any other endeavor, there is talent, there is ingenuity, and there is knowledge. But when all is said and done, what innovation requires is hard, focused, purposeful work. If diligence, persistence, and commitment are lacking, talent, ingenuity, and knowledge are of no avail.

There is, of course, far more to entrepreneurship than systematic innovation—distinct entrepreneurial strategies, for example, and the principles of entrepreneurial management, which are needed equally in the established enterprise, the public service organization, and the new venture. But the very foundation of entrepreneurship is the practice of systematic innovation.

"Nobody Cares
What You Do in There":
The Low Road

STEWART BRAND

It has to do with freedom. Or so I surmised from a 1990 conversation with John Sculley, then head of Apple Computer. Sculley was trained in architecture before he started rocketing up corporate ladders. During a break at a conference, we got talking about buildings. Apple had expanded from five buildings into thirty-one in the few years Sculley had been at Apple. I asked him, "Do you prefer moving into old buildings or making new ones?" "Oh, old ones," he said. "They are much more freeing."

That statement throws a world of design assumptions upside down. *Why* are old buildings more freeing? A way to pursue the question is to ask, what kinds of old buildings are the most freeing?

A young couple moves into an old farmhouse or old barn, lit up with adventure. An entrepreneur opens shop in an echoing warehouse, an artist takes over a drafty loft in the bad part of town, and they feel joy at the prospect. They can't wait to have at the space and put it immediately to work. What these buildings have in common is that they are shabby and spacious. Any change is likely to be an improvement. They are discarded buildings, fairly free of concern from landlord or authorities: "Do what you want. The place can't get much worse anyway. It's just too much trouble to tear down."

Low Road buildings are low-visibility, low-rent, no-style, high-turnover. Most of the world's work is done in Low Road buildings, and even in rich societies the most inventive creativity, especially youthful creativity, will be found in Low Road buildings taking full advantage of the license to try things.

Take MIT—the Massachusetts Institute of Technology. A university campus is ideal for comparing building effectiveness because you have a wide variety of buildings serving a limited number of uses—dormitories, laboratories, classrooms, and offices, that's about it. I'm familiar enough with MIT to know which two buildings are regarded with the most affection among the sixty-eight on campus. One, not surprisingly, is a dormitory called Baker House, designed by Alvar Aalto in 1949. Though Modernist and famous, it is warmly convivial and varied throughout, with a sintered-brick exterior that keeps improving with time.

But the most loved and legendary building of all at MIT is a surprise: a temporary building left over from World War II without even a name, only a number: Building 20. It is a sprawling 250,000 square-foot* three-story wood structure—"The only building on campus you can cut with a saw," says an admirer—

---

* Roughly 25,000 square meters, if you use the rule of thumb: 10 square feet almost equals 1 square meter (0.929 square meters, to be exact).

constructed hastily in 1943 for the urgent development of radar and almost immediately slated for demolition. When I last saw it in 1993, it was still in use and still slated for demolition. In 1978 the MIT Museum assembled an exhibit to honor the perpetual fruitfulness of Building 20. The press release read:

> Unusual flexibility made the building ideal for laboratory and experimental space. Made to support heavy loads and of wood construction, it allowed a use of space which accommodated the enlargement of the working environment either horizontally or vertically. Even the roof was used for short-term structures to house equipment and test instruments.
>
> Although Building 20 was built with the intention to tear it down after the end of World War II, it has remained these thirty-five years providing a special function and acquiring its own history and anecdotes. Not assigned to any one school, department, or center, it seems to always have had space for the beginning project, the graduate student's experiment, the interdisciplinary research center.

Indeed, MIT's first interdisciplinary laboratory, the renowned Research Laboratory of Electronics, founded much of modern communications science there right after the war. The science of linguistics was largely started there, and forty years later in 1993 one of its pioneers, Noam Chomsky, was still rooted there. Innovative labs for the study of nuclear science, cosmic rays, dynamic analysis and control, acoustics, and food technology were born there. Harold Edgerton developed stroboscopic photography there. New-technology companies such as Digital Equipment Corporation and Bolt, Baranek, and Newman incubated

1945: Here photographed from a Navy blimp at the end of World War II, the so-called Radiation Laboratory at Building 20 was one of its unsung heroes. In an undertaking similar in scope to the Manhattan project that created the atomic bomb, the emergency development of radar employed the nation's best physicists in an intense collaboration that changed the nature of science. Unlike Los Alamos, the MIT radar project was not run by the military, and unlike Los Alamos, no secrets got out. The verdict of scientists afterward was, "The atom bomb only ended the war. Radar won it."   THE MIT MUSEUM. NEG. NO. CC-20-417.

1945: During the war the innocuous building at 18 Vassar Street in Cambridge sprouted odd outgrowths overnight.   THE MIT MUSEUM. NEG. NO. CC-20-421.

in Building 20 and later took its informal ways with them into their corporate cultures and headquarters. The Tech Model Railroad Club on the third floor, E Wing, was the source in the early 1960s of most of the first generation of computer "hackers," who set in motion a series of computer technology revolutions (still in progress).

Like most Low Road buildings, Building 20 was too hot in the summer, too cold in the winter, Spartan in its amenities, often dirty, and implacably ugly. Whatever was the attraction? The organizers of the 1978 exhibit queried alumni of the building and got illuminating answers. "Windows that open and shut at will of the owner!" (Martha Ditmeyer) "The ability to personalize your space and shape it to various purposes. If you don't like a wall, just stick your elbow through it." (Jonathan Allan) "If you want to bore a hole in the floor to get a little extra vertical space, you do it. You don't ask. It's the best experimental building ever built." (Albert Hill) "One never needs to worry about injuring the architectural or artistic value of the environment." (Morris Halle) "We feel our space is really ours. We designed it, we run it. The building is full of small microenvironments, each of which is different and each a creative space. Thus the building has a lot of personality. Also it's nice to be in a building that has such prestige." (Heather Lechtman)

In 1991 I asked Jerome Wiesner, retired president of MIT, why he thought that "temporary" Building 20 was still around after half a century. His first answer was practical: "At three hundred dollars a square foot, it would take seventy-five million dollars to replace." His next answer was aesthetic: "It's a very matter-of-fact building. It puts on the personality of the people in it." His final answer was personal. When he was appointed president of the university, he quietly kept a hideaway office in Building 20 because that was where "nobody complained when you nailed something to a door."

Every university has similar stories. Temporary is permanent, and permanent is temporary. Grand, final-solution buildings obsolesce and have to be torn down because they were too over-specified to their original purpose to adapt easily to anything else. Temporary buildings are thrown up quickly and roughly to house temporary projects. Those projects move on soon enough but they are immediately supplanted by other temporary projects— of which, it turns out, there is an endless supply. The projects flourish in the low-supervision environment, free of turf battles because the turf isn't worth fighting over. "We did some of our best work in the trailers, didn't we?" I once heard a Nobel-winning physicist remark. Low Road buildings keep being valuable pre- cisely because they are disposable.

Building 20 raises a question about what are the real ameni- ties. Smart people gave up good heating and cooling, carpeted hallways, big windows, nice views, state-of-the-art construction, and pleasant interior design for what? For sash windows, inter- esting neighbors, strong floors, and freedom.

Many have noticed that young artists flock to rundown indus- trial neighborhoods, and then a predictable sequence occurs. The artists go there for the low rents and plenty of room to mess around. They make the area exciting, and some begin to spruce it up. Eventually it becomes fashionable, with trendy restaurants, nightclubs, and galleries. Real estate values rise to the point where young artists can't afford the higher rents, and the sequence begins again somewhere else. Economic activity follows Low Road activity.

Jane Jacobs explains why:

> Only operations that are well-established, high-turnover, standardized or highly subsidized can afford, commonly, to carry the costs of new construction. Chain stores, chain restaurants, and banks go into new construction. But neighborhood bars, foreign restaurants and pawn shops go into older buildings. Supermarkets and shoe stores often go into new buildings; good bookstores and antique dealers seldom do. Well-subsidized opera and art museums often go into new buildings. But the unformalized feeders of the arts—studios, galleries, stores for musical instruments and art supplies, backrooms where the low earning power of a seat and table can absorb uneconomic discussions—these go into old buildings . . .
>
> Old ideas can sometimes use new buildings. New ideas must come from old buildings.*

A related economic sequence happened around houses. People used to store stuff in basements and attics (big tools and toys in the cellar, clothes and memories in the attic). These were the raw, undifferentiated, Low Roadish parts of the house. But after the 1920s, basements and attics were eschewed by new bungalows, Modernist homes, and ranch houses. Basement storage moved

---

* Jane Jacobs, *The Death and Life of Great American Cities* (New York: Random House, 1961, 1993), p. 245

into the garage, but then it got displaced again when the garage was converted to a studio, home office, spare bedroom, or rental unit. Where did the storage go next? Economic activity followed Low Road activity. The "self-storage" business took off in the 1970s and 1980s. Windowless clusters of garagelike spaces at the edge of town or edge of industrial districts were thrown together and rented out cheap.* In these spaces you find the damnedest things—a boxer working out, quiet adultery, an old gent in a huge chair enjoying a cigar away from his wife, an entire British barn in pieces, a hydroponic garden, stolen goods, a motorcycle repair shop, an artist's studio, someone shaping surfboards, lots of very ordinary storage, and, about once a month somewhere in America, a dead body.

Such trends are invisible to high-style architects, but commercial developers watch them closely. They noticed that small businesses often start up in garages, warehouses, and self-storage spaces, sometimes spawning whole Silicon Valley–type local boomtowns.

When my wife, Patty Phelan, started an equestrian mail order catalogue business, she took over one bay of a huge old wood building left over from World War II—part of a shipyard that had built Liberty ships and tankers. Her bay had all the usual

---

* The Urban Land Institute reported: "With ever-increasing household mobility, a growing national preoccupation with possessions, and escalating demand for low-rent storage spaces (for records, data, and inventory) from businesses and professional offices operating out of relatively high-rent space, demand for self-storage is now equivalent to 2 to 3 square feet per person." "Self-Storage Adaptations," *Urban Land* (Oct. 1991), p.28. In the early 1990s, self-storage facilities were beginning to include climate control, security, multistory buildings, and "acceptable" design on the exterior. It was a $2 billion-a-year industry, complete with its own trade magazine, *Inside Self-Storage*.

amenities—concrete floor, a too-narrow, too-deep space, ill-lit, with a sixty-foot ceiling. She and her staff froze in the winter and baked in the summer. But that space absorbed five years of drastic growth. The company went from one employee to twenty-four, from fifty thousand dollars a year to $3.2 million, while keeping all of its warehousing and shipping on the site. Piece by piece she grew the space, first constructing a second floor, then breaking through a wall into the adjoining bay when that tenant moved out and adding a second floor in there, then cutting through her back wall into some ceilingless interior rooms and roofing them in. Her rent stayed low while she added a skylight, ceiling fans, openable windows, a dutch door, lots more wiring, lots more lighting, and a kitchen.

That's the patterns that developers thought they might be able to duplicate—long, low, cheap building, a series of bays, each with a garage door, low rent, nothing fancy. Called "incubators," they were built by the hundreds, and they prospered. By 1990 there was a National Business Incubation Association boosting another Low Road–derivative industry.

The wonder is that Low Road building use has never been studied formally, either for academic or commercial interest or to tease out design principles that might be useful in other buildings. What do people do to buildings when they can do almost anything they want? I haven't researched the question either, but I've lived some of it. [The book in which this essay appears] was assembled and written in two classic Low Road buildings. My writing office was a derelict landlocked fishing boat named the Mary Heartline. Decades ago, after its fishing career was over, a gay couple acquired it for dockside trysts, fixing it up like a Victorian cottage. Then two divorced gentlemen took it over, also for trysts, but it began sinking, so they moved it onto land, ostensibly for repair. It became a real-estate office, a subscriptions-handling office, and then I got it. It was on no property map of the town. If you leaned against the hull in the wrong place, your hand would go through. It's probably gone by the time you're reading this.

Thanks to the gay couple's Victorian tastes, the place was a maze of little niches, drawers, and cupboards. It was like working inside an old-fashioned rolltop desk. One day I acquired a fax machine. There being no convenient place to park it, I used a saber saw to hack out a level place by the old steering wheel, along with a hole for the electrical and phone lines. It took maybe ten minutes and required no one else's opinion. When you can make adjustments to your space by just picking up a saber saw, you know you're in a Low Road building.

My research library was in a shipping container twenty yards away—one of thirty rented out for self-storage. I got the steel eight-by-eight-by-forty-foot space for $250 a month and spent all of one thousand dollars fixing it up with white paint, cheap carpet, lights, an old couch, and raw plywood work surfaces and shelves. It was heaven. To go in there was to enter the book-in-progress—all the notes, tapes, 5x8 cards, photos, negatives, magazines, articles, 450 books, and other research oddments laid out by chapters or filed carefully. When the summer sun made it too hot for work, I sawed a vent in the wood floor, put a black-painted length of stovepipe out of the ceiling, and slathered the whole top of the container with brightly reflective aluminum paint—end of heat problem. That's how Low Road buildings are made livable: just do it.

In fact, weather becomes a perverse attraction. Whereas competent sealed buildings lull us with their "perfect climate," and incompetent ones drive us crazy with their uncontrollable heats and colds, a drafty old building reminds us what the weather is up to outside and invites us to do something about it—put on a sweater; open a window. Rain is loud on the roof. You smell and feel the seasons. Weather comes in the building a bit. That sort of invasion we would condemn in a new building and blame the architect, but in a ratty old building—designed for some other use after all—there's no one to blame.

Such buildings leave fond memories of improvisation and sensuous delight. When I lived with an artists' commune in an old church in New York State, I slept in the steeple in front of the rose window overlooking the stream below. The major problem was being pooped on by pigeons, so I made a canopy from the canvas of a large bad painting (art side up) and thereafter slept in comfort, cooed to my rest by flights of angels.

Low Road buildings are peculiarly empowering.

How to Kill Creativity

TERESA M. AMABILE

When I consider all the organizations I have studied and worked with over the past twenty-two years, there can be no doubt: creativity gets killed much more often than it gets supported. For the most part, this isn't because managers have a vendetta against creativity. On the contrary, most believe in the value of new and useful ideas. However, creativity is undermined unintentionally every day in work environments that were established—for entirely good reasons—to maximize business imperatives such as coordination, productivity, and control.

Managers cannot be expected to ignore business imperatives, of course. But in acting on these imperatives, they may be inadvertently designing organizations that systematically crush creativity. My research shows that it is possible to develop the best of both worlds: organizations in which business imperatives are attended to and creativity flourishes. Building such organizations, however, requires us to understand precisely what kinds of managerial practices foster creativity—and which kill it.

WHAT IS BUSINESS CREATIVITY?

We tend to associate creativity with the arts and to think of it as the expression of highly original ideas. Think of how Pablo Picasso reworked the conventions of painting or how William Faulkner redefined fiction. In business, originality isn't enough. To be creative, an idea must also be appropriate—useful and actionable. It must somehow influence the way business gets done—by improving a product, for instance, or by opening up a new way to approach a process.

The associations made between creativity and artistic originality often lead to confusion about the appropriate place of creativity in business organizations. In seminars, I've asked managers if there is any place they don't want creativity in their companies. About 80 percent of the time, they answer, "Accounting." Creativity, they seem to believe, belongs just in marketing and R&D. But creativity can benefit every function of an organization. Think of activity-based accounting. It was an invention—an accounting invention—and its impact on business has been positive and profound.

Along with fearing creativity in the accounting department— or really, in any unit that involves systematic processes or legal regulations—many managers also hold a rather narrow view of the creative process. To them, creativity refers to the way people think—how inventively they approach problems, for instance. Indeed, thinking imaginatively is one part of creativity, but two others are also essential: expertise and motivation.

Expertise encompasses everything that a person knows and can do in the broad domain of his or her work. Take, for example, a scientist at a pharmaceutical company who is charged with developing a blood-clotting drug for hemophiliacs. Her expertise includes her basic talent for thinking scientifically as well as all the knowledge and technical abilities that she has in the fields of medicine, chemistry, biology, and biochemistry. It doesn't matter how she acquired this expertise, whether through formal education, practical experience, or interaction with other professionals. Regardless, her expertise constitutes what the Nobel laureate, economist, and psychologist Herb Simon calls her "network of possible wanderings," the intellectual space that she uses to explore and solve problems. The larger this space, the better.

Creative thinking, as noted above, refers to how people approach problems and solutions—their capacity to put existing ideas together in new combinations. The skill itself depends quite a bit on personality as well as on how a person thinks and works. The pharmaceutical scientist, for example, will be more creative if her personality is such that she feels comfortable disagreeing with others—that is, if she naturally tries out solutions that depart from the status quo. Her creativity will be enhanced further if she habitually turns problems upside down and combines knowledge from seemingly disparate fields. For example, she might look to botany to help find solutions to the hemophilia problem, using lessons from the vascular systems of plants to spark insights about bleeding in humans.

As for work style, the scientist will be more likely to achieve creative success if she perseveres through a difficult problem. Indeed, plodding through long dry spells of tedious experimentation increases the probability of truly creative breakthroughs. So, too, does a work style that uses "incubation," the ability to set aside difficult problems temporarily, work on something else, and then return later with a fresh perspective.

Expertise and creative thinking are an individual's raw materials—his or her natural resources, if you will. But a third factor—motivation—determines what people will actually do. The scientist can have outstanding educational credentials and a great facility for generating new perspectives to old problems. But if she lacks the motivation to do a particular job, she simply won't do it; her expertise and creative thinking will either go untapped or be applied to something else.

My research has repeatedly demonstrated, however, that all forms of motivation do not have the same impact on creativity. In fact, it shows that there are two types of motivation—extrinsic and intrinsic, the latter being far more essential for creativity. But let's explore extrinsic first, because it is often at the root of creativity problems in business.

Extrinsic motivation comes from outside a person—whether the motivation is a carrot or a stick. If the scientist's boss promises to reward her financially should the blood-clotting project succeed, or if he threatens to fire her should it fail, she will certainly be motivated to find a solution. But this sort of motivation "makes" the scientist do her job in order to get something desirable or avoid something painful.

Obviously, the most common extrinsic motivator managers use is money, which doesn't necessarily stop people from being creative. But in many situations, it doesn't help either, especially when it leads people to feel that they are being bribed or controlled. More important, money by itself doesn't make employees passionate about their jobs. A cash reward can't magically prompt people to find their work interesting if in their hearts they feel it is dull.

But passion and interest—a person's internal desire to do something—are what intrinsic motivation is all about. For instance, the scientist in our example would be intrinsically motivated if her work on the blood-clotting drug were sparked by an intense interest in hemophilia, a personal sense of challenge, or a drive to crack a problem that no one else has been able to solve. When people are intrinsically motivated, they engage in their work for the challenge and enjoyment of it. The work itself is motivating. In fact, in our creativity research, my students, colleagues, and I have found so much evidence in favor of intrinsic motivation that we have articulated what we call the Intrinsic Motivation Principle of Creativity: people will be most creative when they feel motivated primarily by the interest, satisfaction, and challenge of the work itself—and not by external pressures.

THE CREATIVITY MAZE

To understand the differences between extrinsic and intrinsic motivation, imagine a business problem as a maze.

One person might be motivated to make it through the maze as quickly and safely as possible in order to get a tangible reward, such as money—the same way a mouse would rush through for a piece of cheese. This person would look for the simplest, most straightforward path and then take it. In fact, if he is in a real rush to get that reward, he might just take the most beaten path and solve the problem exactly as it has been solved before.

That approach, based on extrinsic motivation, will indeed get him out of the maze. But the solution that arises from the process is likely to be unimaginative. It won't provide new insights about the nature of the problem or reveal new ways of looking at it. The rote solution probably won't move the business forward.

Another person might have a different approach to the maze. She might actually find the process of wandering around the different paths—the challenge and exploration itself—fun and intriguing. No doubt, this journey will take longer and include mistakes, because any maze—any truly complex problem—has many more dead ends than exits. But when the intrinsically motivated person finally does find a way out of the maze—a solution—it very likely will be more interesting than the rote algorithm. It will be more creative.

There is abundant evidence of strong intrinsic motivation in the stories of widely recognized creative people. When asked what makes the difference between creative scientists and those who are less creative, the Nobel Prize–winning physicist Arthur Schawlow said, "The labor-of-love aspect is important. The most successful scientists often are not the most talented, but the ones who are just impelled by curiosity. They've got to know what the answer is." Albert Einstein talked about intrinsic motivation as "the enjoyment of seeing and searching." The novelist John Irving, in discussing the very long hours he put into his writing, said, "The unspoken factor is love. The reason I can work so hard at my writing is that it's not work for me." And Michael Jordan, perhaps the most creative basketball player ever, had a "love of the game" clause inserted into his contract; he insisted that he be free to play pickup basketball games anytime he wished.

Creative people are rarely superstars like Michael Jordan. Indeed, most of the creative work done in the business world today gets done by people whose names will never be recorded in history books. They are people with expertise, good creative-thinking skills, and high levels of intrinsic motivation. And just as important, they work in organizations where managers consciously build environments that support these characteristics instead of destroying them.

MANAGING CREATIVITY

Managers can influence all three components of creativity: expertise, creative-thinking skills, and motivation. But the fact is that the first two are more difficult and time-consuming to influence than motivation. Yes, regular scientific seminars and professional conferences will undoubtedly add to the scientist's expertise in hemophilia and related fields. And training in brainstorming, problem solving, and so-called lateral thinking might give her some new tools to use in tackling the job. But the time and money involved in broadening her knowledge and expanding her creative-thinking skills would be great. By contrast, our research has shown that intrinsic motivation can be increased considerably by even subtle changes in an organization's environment. That is not to say that managers should give up on improving expertise and creative-thinking skills. But when it comes to pulling levers, they should know that those that affect intrinsic motivation will yield more immediate results.

More specifically, then, what managerial practices affect creativity? They fall into six general categories: challenge, freedom, resources, work-group features, supervisory encouragement, and organizational support. These categories have emerged from more than two decades of research focused primarily on one question: what are the links between work environment and creativity? We have used three methodologies: experiments, interviews, and surveys. While controlled experiments allowed us to identify causal links, the interviews and surveys gave us insight into the richness and complexity of creativity within business organizations. We have studied dozens of companies and, within those, hundreds of individuals and teams. In each research initiative, our goal has been to identify which managerial practices are definitively linked to positive creative outcomes and which are not.

For instance, in one project, we interviewed dozens of employees from a wide variety of companies and industries and asked them to describe in detail the most and least creative events in their careers. We then closely studied the transcripts of those interviews, noting the managerial practices—or other patterns—that appeared repeatedly in the successful creativity stories and, conversely, in those that were unsuccessful. Our research has also been bolstered by a quantitative survey instrument called KEYS. Taken by employees at any level of an organization, KEYS consists of seventy-eight questions used to assess various workplace conditions, such as the level of support for creativity from top-level managers or the organization's approach to evaluation.

Taking the six categories that have emerged from our research in turn, let's explore what managers can do to enhance creativity—and what often happens instead. Again, it is important to note that creativity-killing practices are seldom the work of lone managers. Such practices usually are systemic—so widespread that they are rarely questioned.

Challenge

Of all the things managers can do to stimulate creativity, perhaps the most efficacious is the deceptively simple task of matching people with the right assignments. Managers can match people with jobs that play to their expertise and their skills in creative thinking, and ignite intrinsic motivation. Perfect matches stretch employees' abilities. The amount of stretch, however, is crucial: not so little that they feel bored but not so much that they feel overwhelmed and threatened by a loss of control.

Making a good match requires that managers possess rich and detailed information about their employees and the available assignments. Such information is often difficult and time-consuming to gather. Perhaps that's why good matches are so rarely made. In fact, one of the most common ways managers kill creativity is by not trying to obtain the information necessary to make good connections between people and jobs. Instead, something of a shotgun wedding occurs. The most eligible employee is wed to the most eligible—that is, the most urgent and open—

assignment. Often, the results are predictably unsatisfactory for all involved.

Freedom

When it comes to granting freedom, the key to creativity is giving people autonomy concerning the means—that is, concerning process—but not necessarily the ends. People will be more creative, in other words, if you give them freedom to decide how to climb a particular mountain. You needn't let them choose which mountain to climb. In fact, clearly specified strategic goals often enhance people's creativity.

I'm not making the case that managers should leave their subordinates entirely out of goal- or agenda-setting discussions. But they should understand that inclusion in those discussions will not necessarily enhance creative output and certainly will not be sufficient to do so. It is far more important that whoever sets the goals also makes them clear to the organization and that these goals remain stable for a meaningful period of time. It is difficult, if not impossible, to work creatively toward a target if it keeps moving.

Autonomy around process fosters creativity because giving people freedom in how they approach their work heightens their intrinsic motivation and sense of ownership. Freedom about process also allows people to approach problems in ways that make the most of their expertise and their creative-thinking skills. The task may end up being a stretch for them, but they can use their strengths to meet the challenge.

How do executives mismanage freedom? There are two common ways. First, managers tend to change goals frequently or fail to define them clearly. Employees may have freedom around process, but if they don't know where they are headed, such freedom is pointless. And second, some managers fall short on this dimension by granting autonomy in name only. They claim that employees are "empowered" to explore the maze as they search for solutions but, in fact, the process is proscribed. Employees diverge at their own risk.

Resources

The two main resources that affect creativity are time and money. Managers need to allot these resources carefully. Like matching people with the right assignments, deciding how much time and money to give to a team or project is a sophisticated judgment call that can either support or kill creativity.

Consider time. Under some circumstances, time pressure can heighten creativity. Say, for instance, that a competitor is about to launch a great product at a lower price than you're offering or that society faces a serious problem and desperately needs a solution—such as an AIDS vaccine. In such situations, both the time crunch and the importance of the work legitimately make people feel that they must rush. Indeed, cases like these would be apt to increase intrinsic motivation by increasing the sense of challenge.

Organizations routinely kill creativity with fake deadlines or impossibly tight ones. The former create distrust and the latter cause burnout. In either case, people feel overcontrolled and unfulfilled—which invariably damages motivation. Moreover, creativity often takes time. It can be slow going to explore new concepts, put together unique solutions, and wander through the maze. Managers who do not allow time for exploration or do not schedule in incubation periods are unwittingly standing in the way of the creative process.

When it comes to project resources, again managers must make a fit. They must determine the funding, people, and other resources that a team legitimately needs to complete an assignment—and they must know how much the organization can legitimately afford to allocate to the assignment. Then they must strike a compromise. Interestingly, adding more resources above a "threshold of sufficiency" does not boost creativity. Below that threshold, however, a restriction of resources can dampen creativity. Unfortunately, many managers don't realize this and therefore often make another mistake. They keep resources tight, which pushes people to channel their creativity into finding additional resources, not in actually developing new products or services.

Another resource that is misunderstood when it comes to creativity is physical space. It is almost conventional wisdom that creative teams need open, comfortable offices. Such an atmosphere won't hurt creativity, and it may even help, but it is not nearly as important as other managerial initiatives that influence creativity. Indeed, a problem we have seen time and time again is managers paying attention to creating the "right" physical space at the expense of more high-impact actions, such as matching people to the right assignments and granting freedom around work processes.

Work-Group Features

If you want to build teams that come up with creative ideas, you must pay careful attention to the design of such teams. That is, you must create mutually supportive groups with a diversity of perspectives and backgrounds. Why? Because when teams comprise people with various intellectual foundations and approaches to work—that is, different expertise and creative thinking styles— ideas often combine and combust in exciting and useful ways.

Diversity, however, is only a starting point. Managers must also make sure that the teams they put together have three other features. First, the members must share excitement over the team's goal. Second, members must display a willingness to help their teammates through difficult periods and setbacks. And third, every member must recognize the unique knowledge and perspective that other members bring to the table. These factors enhance not only intrinsic motivation but also expertise and creative-thinking skills.

Again, creating such teams requires managers to have a deep understanding of their people. They must be able to assess them not just for their knowledge but for their attitudes about potential fellow team members and the collaborative process, for their problem-solving styles, and for their motivational hot buttons. Putting together a team with just the right chemistry—just the right level of diversity and supportiveness—can be difficult, but our research shows how powerful it can be.

It follows, then, that one common way managers kill creativity is by assembling homogeneous teams. The lure to do so is great. Homogeneous teams often reach "solutions" more quickly and with less friction along the way. These teams often report high morale, too. But homogeneous teams do little to enhance expertise and creative thinking. Everyone comes to the table with a similar mind-set. They leave with the same.

Supervisory Encouragement

Most managers are extremely busy. They are under pressure for results. It is therefore easy for them to let praise for creative efforts—not just creative successes but unsuccessful efforts, too—fall by the wayside. One very simple step managers can take to foster creativity is not to let that happen.

The connection to intrinsic motivation here is clear. Certainly, people can find their work interesting or exciting without a cheering section—for some period of time. But to sustain such passion, most people need to feel as if their work matters to the organization or to some important group of people. Otherwise, they might as well do their work at home and for their own personal gain.

Managers in successful, creative organizations rarely offer specific extrinsic rewards for particular outcomes. However, they freely and generously recognize creative work by individuals and teams—often before the ultimate commercial impact of those efforts is known. By contrast, managers who kill creativity do so either by failing to acknowledge innovative efforts or by greeting them with skepticism. In many companies, for instance, new ideas are met not with open minds but with time-consuming layers of evaluation—or even with harsh criticism. When someone suggests a new product or process, senior managers take weeks to respond. Or they put that person through an excruciating critique.

Not every new idea is worthy of consideration, of course, but in many organizations, managers habitually demonstrate a reaction that damages creativity. They look for reasons not to use a new idea instead of searching for reasons to explore it further. An interesting psychological dynamic underlies this phenomenon. Our research shows that people believe that they will appear smarter to their bosses if they are more critical—and it often works. In many organizations, it is professionally rewarding to react critically to new ideas.

Unfortunately, this sort of negativity bias can have severe consequences for the creativity of those being evaluated. How? First, a culture of evaluation leads people to focus on the external rewards and punishments associated with their output, thus increasing the presence of extrinsic motivation and its potentially negative effects on intrinsic motivation. Second, such a culture creates a climate of fear, which again undermines intrinsic motivation.

Finally, negativity also shows up in how managers treat people whose ideas don't pan out: often, they are terminated or otherwise warehoused within the organization. Of course, ultimately, ideas do need to work; remember that creative ideas in business must be new and useful. The dilemma is that you can't possibly know beforehand which ideas will pan out. Furthermore, dead ends can sometimes be very enlightening. In many business situations, knowing what doesn't work can be as useful as knowing what does. But if people do not perceive any "failure value" for projects that ultimately do not achieve commercial success, they'll become less and less likely to experiment, explore, and connect with their work on a personal level. Their intrinsic motivation will evaporate.

Supervisory encouragement comes in other forms besides rewards and punishment. Another way managers can support creativity is to serve as role models, persevering through tough problems as well as encouraging collaboration and communication within the team. Such behavior enhances all three components of the creative process, and it has the added virtue of being a high-impact practice that a single manager can take on his or her own. It is better still when all managers in an organization serve as role models for the attitudes and behaviors that encourage and nurture creativity.

Organizational Support

Encouragement from supervisors certainly fosters creativity, but creativity is truly enhanced when the entire organization supports it. Such support is the job of an organization's leaders, who must put in place appropriate systems or procedures and emphasize values that make it clear that creative efforts are a top priority. For example, creativity-supporting organizations consistently reward creativity, but they avoid using money to "bribe" people to come up with innovative ideas. Because monetary rewards make people feel as if they are being controlled, such a tactic probably won't work. At the same time, not providing sufficient recognition and rewards for creativity can spawn negative feelings within an organization. People can feel used, or at the least

underappreciated, for their creative efforts. And it is rare to find
the energy and passion of intrinsic motivation coupled with resentment.

Most important, an organization's leaders can support creativity by mandating information sharing and collaboration and
by ensuring that political problems do not fester. Information
sharing and collaboration support all three components of creativity. Take expertise. The more often people exchange ideas
and data by working together, the more knowledge they will
have. The same dynamic can be said for creative thinking. In fact,
one way to enhance the creative thinking of employees is to ex-
pose them to various approaches to problem solving. With the
exception of hardened misanthropes, information sharing and
collaboration heighten people's enjoyment of work and thus their
intrinsic motivation.

Whether or not you are seeking to enhance creativity, it is
probably never a good idea to let political problems fester in an
organizational setting. Infighting, politicking, and gossip are
particularly damaging to creativity because they take people's attention away from work. That sense of mutual purpose and excitement so central to intrinsic motivation invariably lessens
when people are cliquish or at war with one another. Indeed, our
research suggests that intrinsic motivation increases when people
are aware that those around them are excited by their jobs. When
political problems abound, people feel that their work is threatened by others' agendas.

Finally, politicking also undermines expertise. The reason?
Politics get in the way of open communication, obstructing the
flow of information from point A to point B. Knowledge stays
put and expertise suffers.

FROM THE INDIVIDUAL TO THE ORGANIZATION

Can executives build entire organizations that support creativity? The answer is yes. Consider the results of an intensive research project we recently completed called the Team Events Study. Over the course of two years, we studied more than two dozen teams in seven companies across three industries: high tech, consumer products, and chemicals. By following each team every day through the entire course of a creative project, we had a window into the details of what happened as the project progressed—or failed to progress, as the case may be. We did this through daily confidential e-mail reports from every person on each of the teams. At the end of each project, and at several points along the way, we used confidential reports from company experts and from team members to assess the level of creativity used in problem solving as well as the overall success of the project.

As might be expected, the teams and the companies varied widely in how successful they were at producing creative work. One organization, which I will call Chemical Central Research, seemed to be a veritable hotbed of creativity. Chemical Central supplied its parent organization with new formulations for a wide variety of industrial and consumer products. In many respects, however, members of Chemical Central's development teams were unremarkable. They were well educated, but no more so than people in many other companies we had studied. The company was doing well financially, but not enormously better than most other companies. What seemed to distinguish this organization was the quality of leadership at both the top-management level and the team level. The way managers formed teams, com-

The Three Components of Creativity

Within every individual, creativity is a function of three components: expertise, creative-thinking skills, and motivation. Can managers influence these components? The answer is an emphatic yes—for better or for worse—through workplace practices and conditions.

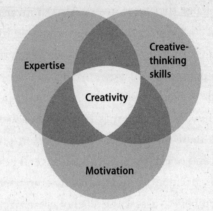

Expertise is, in a word, knowledge—technical, procedural, and intellectual.

Creative-thinking skills determine how flexibly and imaginatively people approach problems. Do their solutions upend the status quo? Do they persevere through dry spells?

Not all **motivation** is created equal. An inner passion to solve the problem at hand leads to solutions far more creative than do external rewards, such as money. This component—called *intrinsic motivation*—is the one that can be more immediately influenced by the work environment.

municated with them, and supported their work enabled them to establish an organization in which creativity was continually stimulated.

We saw managers making excellent matches between people and assignments again and again at Chemical Central. On occasion, team members were initially unsure of whether they were up to the challenge they were given. Almost invariably, though, they found their passion and interest growing through a deep involvement in the work. Their managers knew to match them with jobs that had them working at the top of their competency levels, pushing the frontiers of their skills, and developing new competencies. But managers were careful not to allow too big a gap between employees' assignments and their abilities.

Moreover, managers at Chemical Central collaborated with the teams from the outset of a project to clarify goals. The final goals, however, were set by the managers. Then, at the day-to-day operational level, the teams were given a great deal of autonomy to make their own decisions about product development. Throughout the project, the teams' leaders and top-level managers periodically checked to see that work was directed toward the overall goals. But people were given real freedom around the implementation of the goals.

As for work-group design, every Chemical Central team, though relatively small (between four and nine members), included members of diverse professional and ethnic backgrounds. Occasionally, that diversity led to communication difficulties. But more often it sparked new insights and allowed the teams to come up with a wider variety of ways to accomplish their goals.

One team, for example, was responsible for devising a new way to make a major ingredient for one of the company's most important products. Because managers at Chemical Central had worked consciously to create a diverse team, it happened that one member had both a legal and a technical background. This person realized that the team might well be able to patent its core idea, giving the company a clear advantage in a new market. Because team members were mutually supportive, that member was willing and eager to work closely with the inventor. Together, these individuals helped the team navigate its way through the patent application process. The team was successful and had fun along the way.

Supervisory encouragement and organizational support were also widespread at Chemical Central. For instance, a member of one team received a company award as an outstanding scientist even though, along the way, he had experienced many failures as well as successes. At one point, after spending a great deal of time on one experiment, he told us, "All I came up with was a pot of junk." Still, the company did not punish or warehouse him because of a creative effort that had failed. Instead, he was publicly lauded for his consistently creative work.

Finally, Chemical Central's leaders did much to encourage teams to seek support from all units within their divisions and to encourage collaboration across all quarters. The general manager of the research unit himself set an example, offering both strategic and technical ideas whenever teams approached him for help. Indeed, he explicitly made cross-team support a priority among top scientists in the organization. As a result, such support was expected and recognized.

For example, one team was about to test a new formulation for one of the company's major products. Because the team was small, it had to rely on a materials-analysis group within the organization to help conduct the tests. The analysis group not only helped out but also set aside generous blocks of time during the week before testing to help the team understand the nature and limits of the information the group would provide, when they would have it, and what they would need from the team to support them effectively. Members of the team were confident that they could rely on the materials-analysis group throughout the process, and the trials went well—despite the usual technical difficulties encountered in such testing.

By contrast, consider what we observed at another company in our study, a consumer products company we'll call National Houseware Products. For years, National had been well known for its innovation. But recently, the company had been restructured to accommodate a major growth spurt, and many senior managers had been fired or transferred. National's work environment had undergone drastic changes. At the same time new product successes and new business ideas seemed to be slowing to a trickle. Interestingly, the daily reports of the Team Events Study revealed that virtually all creativity killers were present.

Managers undermined autonomy by continually changing goals and interfering with processes. At one quarterly review meeting, for example, four priorities that had been defined by management at the previous quarterly review meeting were not even mentioned. In another instance, a product that had been identified as the team's number one project was suddenly dropped without explanation.

Resources were similarly mismanaged. For instance, management perennially put teams under severe and seemingly arbitrary time and resource constraints. At first, many team members were energized by the firefighting atmosphere. They threw themselves into their work and rallied. But after a few months, their verve had diminished, especially because the pressures had proved meaningless.

But perhaps National's managers damaged creativity most with their approach to evaluation. They were routinely critical of new suggestions. One employee told us that he was afraid to tell his managers about some radical ideas that he had developed to grow his area of the business. The employee was wildly enthusiastic about the potential for his ideas but ultimately didn't mention them to any of his bosses. He wondered why he should bother talking about new ideas when each one was studied for all its flaws instead of its potential. Through its actions, management had too often sent the message that any big ideas about how to change the status quo would be carefully scrutinized. Those individuals brave enough to suggest new ideas had to endure long—often nasty—meetings, replete with suspicious questions.

In another example, when a team took a new competitive pricing program to the boss, it was told that a discussion of the idea would have to wait another month. One exasperated team member noted, "We analyze so long, we've lost the business before we've taken any action at all!"

Yet another National team had put in particularly long hours over a period of several weeks to create a radically improved version of a major product. The team succeeded in bringing out the product on time and in budget, and it garnered promising market response. But management acted as if everything were business as usual, providing no recognition or reward to the team. A couple of months later, when we visited the team to report the results of our study, we learned that the team leader had just accepted a job from a smaller competitor. He confided that although he felt that the opportunities for advancement and ultimate visibility may have been greater at National, he believed his work and his ideas would be valued more highly somewhere else.

And finally, the managers at National allowed political problems to fester. Consider the time a National team came up with a great idea to save money in manufacturing a new product—which was especially urgent because a competitor had just come out with a similar product at a lower price. The plan was nixed. As a matter of "policy"—a code word for long-held allegiances and rivalries within the company—the manufacturing division wouldn't allow it. One team member commented, "If facts and figures instead of politics reigned supreme, this would be a no-brainer. There are no definable cost savings from running the products where they do, and there is no counterproposal on how to save the money another way. It's just 'No!' because this is the way they want it."

GREAT REWARDS AND RISKS

The important lesson of the National and Chemical Central stories is that fostering creativity is in the hands of managers as they think about, design, and establish the work environment. Creativity often requires that managers radically change the ways in which they build and interact with work groups. In many respects, it calls for a conscious culture change. But it can be done, and the rewards can be great.

The risks of not doing so may be even greater. When creativity is killed, an organization loses a potent competitive weapon:

new ideas. It can also lose the energy and commitment of its people. Indeed, in all my years of research into creativity, perhaps the most difficult part has been hearing people complain that they feel stifled, frustrated, and shut down by their organizations. As one team member at National told us, "By the time I get home every day, I feel physically, emotionally, and intellectually drained. Help!"

Even if organizations seemed trapped in organizational ecosystems that kill creativity—as in the case of National Houseware Products—it is still possible to effect widespread change. Consider a recent transformation at Procter & Gamble. Once a hotbed of creativity, P&G had in recent years seen the number of its product innovations decline significantly. In response, the company established Corporate New Ventures (CNV), a small cross-functional team that embodies many of the creativity-enhancing practices described in this article.

In terms of challenge, for instance, members of the CNV team were allowed to elect themselves. How better to make sure someone is intrinsically motivated for an assignment than to ask for volunteers? Building a team from volunteers, it should be noted, was a major departure from standard P&G procedures. Members of the CNV team also were given a clear, challenging strategic goal: to invent radical new products that would build the company's future. Again departing from typical P&G practices, the team was given enormous latitude around how, when, and where they approached their work.

The list of the ways that CNV broke with P&G's creativity-killing practices is a long one. On nearly every creativity-support dimension in the KEYS work-environment survey, CNV scored higher than national norms and higher than the pre-CNV environment at P&G. But more important than the particulars is the question: has the changed environment resulted in more creative work? Undeniably so, and the evidence is convincing. In the three years since its inception, CNV has handed off eleven projects to the business sectors for execution. And as of early 1998, those products were beginning to flow out of the pipeline. The first product, designed to provide portable heat for several hours' relief of minor pain, was already in test marketing. And six other products were slated to go to test market within a year. Not surprisingly, given CNV's success, P&G is beginning to expand both the size and the scope of its CNV venture.

Even if you believe that your organization fosters creativity, take a hard look for creativity killers. Some of them may be flourishing in a dark corner—or even in the light. But rooting out creativity-killing behaviors isn't enough. You have to make a conscious effort to support creativity. The result can be a truly innovative company where creativity doesn't just survive but actually thrives.

The Rise of
the Creative Class

Why Cities Without Gays and Rock Bands Are
Losing the Economic Development Race

RICHARD FLORIDA

As I walked across the campus of Pittsburgh's Carnegie Mellon University one delightful spring day, I came upon a table filled with young people chatting and enjoying the spectacular weather. Several had identical blue T-shirts with "Trilogy@CMU" written across them—Trilogy being an Austin, Texas–based software company with a reputation for recruiting our top students. I walked over to the table. "Are you guys here to recruit?" I asked. "No, absolutely not," they replied adamantly. "We're not recruiters. We're just hangin' out, playing a little Frisbee with our friends." How interesting, I thought. They've come to campus on a workday, all the way from Austin, just to hang out with some new friends.

I noticed one member of the group sitting slouched over on the grass, dressed in a tank top. This young man had spiked multicolored hair, full-body tattoos, and multiple piercings in his ears. An obvious slacker, I thought, probably in a band. "So what is your story?" I asked. "Hey man, I just signed on with these guys." In fact, as I would later learn, he was a gifted student who had inked the highest-paying deal of any graduating student in the history of his department, right at that table on the grass, with the recruiters who do not "recruit."

What a change from my own college days, just a little more than twenty years ago, when students would put on their dressiest clothes and carefully hide any counterculture tendencies to prove that they could fit in with the company. Today, apparently, it's the company trying to fit in with the students. In fact, Trilogy had wined and dined him over margarita parties in Pittsburgh and flown him to Austin for private parties in hip nightspots and aboard company boats. When I called the people who had recruited him to ask why, they answered, "That's easy. We wanted him because he's a rock star."

While I was interested in the change in corporate recruiting strategy, something even bigger struck me. Here was another example of a talented young person leaving Pittsburgh. Clearly, my adopted hometown has a huge number of assets. Carnegie Mellon is one of the world's leading centers for research in information technology. The University of Pittsburgh, right down the street from our campus, has a world-class medical center. Pittsburgh attracts hundreds of millions of dollars per year in university research funding and is the sixth-largest center for college and university students on a per capita basis in the country. Moreover, the city is hardly a cultural backwater. It is home to three major sports franchises, renowned museums and cultural venues, a spectacular network of urban parks, fantastic industrial-age architecture, and great urban neighborhoods with an abundance of charming yet affordable housing. It is a friendly city, defined by strong communities and a strong sense of pride. In the 1986 Rand McNally survey, Pittsburgh was ranked "America's Most Livable City," and has continued to score high on such lists ever since.

Yet Pittsburgh's economy continues to putter along in a middling flatline pattern. Both the core city and the surrounding metropolitan area lost population in the 2000 census. And those bright young university people keep leaving. Most of Carnegie Mellon's prominent alumni of recent years—like Vinod Khosla, perhaps the best known of Silicon Valley's venture capitalists, and Rick Rashid, head of research and development at Microsoft—went elsewhere to make their marks. Pitt's vaunted medical center, where Jonas Salk created his polio vaccine and the world's premier organ-transplant program was started, has inspired only a handful of entrepreneurs to build biotech companies in Pittsburgh.

Over the years, I have seen the community try just about everything possible to remake itself so as to attract and retain talented young people, and I was personally involved in many of these efforts. Pittsburgh has launched a multitude of programs to diversify the region's economy away from heavy industry into high technology. It has rebuilt its downtown virtually from scratch, invested in a new airport, and developed a massive new sports complex for the Pirates and the Steelers. But nothing, it seemed, could stem the tide of people and new companies leaving the region.

I asked the young man with the spiked hair why he was going

to a smaller city in the middle of Texas, a place with a small air-port and no professional sports teams, without a major symphony, ballet, opera, or art museum comparable to Pittsburgh's. The company is excellent, he told me. There are also terrific people and the work is challenging. But the clincher, he said, is that "It's in Austin!" There are lots of young people, he went on to explain, and a tremendous amount to do: a thriving music scene, ethnic and cultural diversity, fabulous outdoor recreation, and great nightlife. Though he had several good job offers from Pittsburgh high-tech firms and knew the city well, he said he felt it lacked the lifestyle options, cultural diversity, and tolerant attitude that would make it attractive to him. As he summed it up: "How would I fit in here?"

This young man and his lifestyle proclivities represent a profound new force in the economy and life of America. He is a member of what I call the creative class: a fast-growing, highly educated, and well-paid segment of the workforce on whose efforts corporate profits and economic growth increasingly depend. Members of the creative class do a wide variety of work in a wide variety of industries—from technology to entertainment, journalism to finance, high-end manufacturing to the arts. They do not consciously think of themselves as a class. Yet they share a common ethos that values creativity, individuality, difference, and merit.

More and more businesses understand that ethos and are making the adaptations necessary to attract and retain creative-class employees—everything from relaxed dress codes, flexible schedules, and new work rules in the office to hiring recruiters who throw Frisbees. Most civic leaders, however, have failed to understand that what is true for corporations is also true for cities and regions: places that succeed in attracting and retaining creative class people prosper; those that fail don't.

Stuck in old paradigms of economic development, cities like Buffalo, New Orleans, and Louisville struggled in the 1980s and

---

The Creativity Index
(Guide to Charts)

The key to economic growth lies not just in the ability to attract the creative class, but to translate that underlying advantage into creative economic outcomes in the form of new ideas, new high-tech businesses, and regional growth. To better gauge these capabilities, I developed a new measure called the Creativity Index (column 1). The Creativity Index is a mix of four equally weighted factors: the creative-class share of the workforce (column 2 shows the percentage; column 3 ranks cities accordingly); high-tech industry, using the Milken Institute's widely accepted Tech Pole Index, which I refer to as the High-Tech Index (column 4); innovation, measured as patents per capita (column 5); and diversity, measured by the Gay Index, a reasonable proxy for an area's openness to different kinds of people and ideas (column 6). This composite indicator is a better measure of a region's underlying creative capabilities than the simple measure of the creative class, because it reflects the joint effects of its concentration and of innovative economic outcomes. The Creativity Index is thus my baseline indicator of a region's overall standing in the creative economy and I offer it as a barometer of a region's longer-run economic potential. The following tables present my Creativity Index ranking for the top ten and bottom ten metropolitan areas, grouped into three size categories (large, medium size, and small cities/regions).

Large Cities Creativity Rankings

Rankings of 49 metro areas reporting populations
over 1 million in the 2000 Census

TOP TEN CITIES

City	Creativity Index	% Creative Workers	Creative Rank	High-Tech Rank	Innovation Rank	Diversity Rank
1. San Francisco	1057	34.8	5	1	2	1
2. Austin	1028	36.4	4	11	3	16
3. San Diego	1015	32.1	15	12	7	3
3. Boston	1015	38.0	3	2	6	22
5. Seattle	1008	32.7	9	3	12	8
6. Chapel Hill	996	38.2	2	14	4	28
7. Houston	980	32.5	10	16	16	10
8. Washington	964	38.4	1	5	30	12
9. New York	962	32.3	12	13	24	14
10. Dallas	960	30.2	23	6	17	9
10. Minneapolis	960	33.9	7	21	5	29

BOTTOM TEN CITIES

City	Creativity Index	% Creative Workers	Creative Rank	High-Tech Rank	Innovation Rank	Diversity Rank
49. Memphis	530	24.8	47	48	42	41
48. Norfolk, VA	555	28.4	36	35	49	47
47. Las Vegas	561	18.5	49	42	47	5
46. Buffalo	609	28.9	33	40	27	49
45. Louisville	622	26.5	46	46	39	36
44. Grand Rapids	639	24.3	48	43	23	38
43. Oklahoma City	668	29.4	29	41	43	39
42. New Orleans	668	27.5	42	45	48	13
41. Greensboro	697	27.3	44	33	35	35
40. Providence	698	27.6	41	44	34	33

1990s to become the next "Silicon Somewhere" by building generic high-tech office parks or subsidizing professional sports teams. Yet they lost members of the creative class, and their economic dynamism, to places like Austin, Boston, Washington, D.C., and Seattle—places more tolerant, diverse, and open to creativity. Because of this migration of the creative class, a new social and economic geography is emerging in America, one that does not correspond to old categories like East Coast versus West Coast or Sunbelt versus Frostbelt. Rather, it is more like the class divisions that have increasingly separated Americans by income and neighborhood, extended into the realm of city and region.

THE CREATIVE SECRETARY

The distinguishing characteristic of the creative class is that its members engage in work whose function is to "create meaningful new forms." The supercreative core of this new class includes scientists and engineers, university professors, poets and novelists, artists, entertainers, actors, designers, and architects, as well as the "thought leadership" of modern society: nonfiction writers, editors, cultural figures, think-tank researchers, analysts, and other opinion makers. Members of this supercreative core produce new forms or designs that are readily transferable and broadly useful—such as designing a product that can be widely made, sold, and used; coming up with a theorem or strategy that can be applied in many cases; or composing music that can be performed again and again.

Beyond this core group, the creative class also includes "creative professionals" who work in a wide range of knowledge-intensive industries such as high-tech sectors, financial services, the legal and health care professions, and business management. These people engage in creative problem solving, drawing on complex bodies of knowledge to solve specific problems. Doing so typically requires a high degree of formal education and thus a high level of human capital. People who do this kind of work may sometimes come up with methods or products that turn out to be widely useful, but it's not part of the basic job description. What they are required to do regularly is think on their own. They apply or combine standard approaches in unique ways to fit the situation, exercise a great deal of judgment, perhaps try something radically new from time to time.

Much the same is true of the growing number of technicians and others who apply complex bodies of knowledge to working with physical materials. In fields such as medicine and scientific research, technicians are taking on increased responsibility to interpret their work and make decisions, blurring the old distinction between white-collar work (done by decision makers) and blue-collar work (done by those who follow orders). They acquire their own arcane bodies of knowledge and develop their own unique ways of doing the job. Another example is the secretary in today's pared-down offices. In many cases, this person not only takes on a host of tasks once performed by a large secretarial staff, but becomes a true office manager—channeling flows of information, devising and setting up new systems, often making key decisions on the fly. These people contribute more than intelligence or computer skills. They add creative value. Everywhere we look, creativity is increasingly valued. Firms and organizations

Medium-Size Cities Creativity Rankings

Rankings of 32 metro areas reporting populations
500,000 to 1 million in the 2000 Census

TOP TEN CITIES

City	Creativity Index	% Creative Workers	Creative Rank	High-Tech Rank	Innovation Rank	Diversity Rank
1. Albuquerque	965	32.2	2	1	7	1
2. Albany, NY	932	33.7	1	12	2	4
3. Tuscon, AZ	853	28.4	17	2	6	5
4. Allentown, PA	801	28.7	16	13	3	14
5. Dayton, OH	766	30.1	8	8	5	24
6. Colorado Springs	756	29.9	10	5	1	30
7. Harrisburg, PA	751	29.8	11	6	13	20
8. Little Rock, AR	740	30.8	4	10	21	11
9. Birmingham, AL	722	30.7	6	7	26	10
10. Tulsa, OK	721	28.7	15	9	15	18

BOTTOM TEN CITIES

City	Creativity Index	% Creative Workers	Creative Rank	High-Tech Rank	Innovation Rank	Diversity Rank
32. Youngstown, OH	253	23.8	32	32	24	32
31. Scranton, PA	400	24.7	28	23	23	31
30. McAllen, TX	451	27.8	18	31	32	9
29. Stockton, CA	459	24.1	30	29	28	7
28. El Paso, TX	464	27.0	23	27	31	17
27. Fresno, CA	516	25.1	27	24	30	2
26. Bakersfield, CA	531	27.8	18	22	27	19
25. Fort Wayne, IN	569	25.4	26	17	8	26
24. Springfield, MA	577	29.7	13	30	20	22
23. Honolulu, HI	580	27.2	21	14	29	6

value it for the results that it can produce and individuals value it as a route to self-expression and job satisfaction. Bottom line: as creativity becomes more valued, the creative class grows.

The creative class now includes some 38.3 million Americans, roughly 30 percent of the entire U.S. workforce—up from just 10 percent at the turn of the twentieth century and less than 20 percent as recently as 1980. The creative class has considerable economic power. In 1999, the average salary for a member of the creative class was nearly $50,000 ($48,752), compared to roughly $28,000 for a working-class member and $22,000 for a service-class worker.

Not surprisingly, regions that have large numbers of creative-class members are also some of the most affluent and growing.

THE NEW GEOGRAPHY OF CLASS

Different classes of people have long sorted themselves into neighborhoods within a city or region. But now we find a large-scale re-sorting of people among cities and regions nationwide, with some regions becoming centers of the creative class while others are composed of larger shares of working-class or service-class people. To some extent this has always been true. For instance, there have always been artistic and cultural communities like Greenwich Village, college towns like Madison and Boulder, and manufacturing centers like Pittsburgh and Detroit. The news is that such sorting is becoming even more widespread and pronounced.

In the leading centers of this new class geography, the creative class makes up more than 35 percent of the workforce. This is already the case in the greater Washington, D.C., region, the Raleigh-Durham area, Boston, and Austin—all areas undergoing tremendous economic growth. Despite their considerable advantages, large regions have not cornered the market as creative-class locations. In fact, a number of smaller regions have some of the highest creative-class concentrations in the nation— notably college towns like East Lansing, Michigan, and Madison, Wisconsin.

At the other end of the spectrum are regions that are being bypassed by the creative class. Among large regions, Las Vegas, Grand Rapids, and Memphis harbor the smallest concentrations of the creative class. Members of this class have nearly abandoned a wide range of smaller regions in the outskirts of the South and Midwest. In small metropolitan areas like Victoria, Texas, and Jackson, Tennessee, the creative class composes less than 15 percent of the workforce. The leading centers for the working class among large regions are Greensboro, North Carolina, and Memphis, Tennessee, where the working class makes up more than 30 percent of the workforce. Several smaller regions in the South and Midwest are veritable working-class enclaves with 40 to 50 percent or more of their workforce in the traditional industrial occupations.

These places have some of the most minuscule concentrations of the creative class in the nation. They are symptomatic of a general lack of overlap between the major creative-class centers and those of the working class. Of the twenty-six large cities where the working class composes more than one-quarter of the population, only one, Houston, ranks among the top ten destinations for the creative class.

Chicago, a bastion of working-class people that still ranks among the top twenty large creative centers, is interesting because it shows how the creative class and the traditional working class can coexist. But Chicago has an advantage in that it is a big city, with more than a million members of the creative class. The University of Chicago sociologist Terry Clark likes to say Chicago developed an innovative political and cultural solution to this issue. Under the second Mayor Daley, the city integrated the members of the creative class into its culture and politics by treating them essentially as just another "ethnic group" that needed sufficient space to express its identity.

Las Vegas has the highest concentration of the service class among large cities, 58 percent, while West Palm Beach, Orlando, and Miami also have around half. These regions rank near the bottom of the list for the creative class. The service class makes up more than half the workforce in nearly fifty small and medium-size regions across the country. Few of them boast any significant concentrations of the creative class, save vacationers, and offer little prospect for upward mobility. They include resort towns like Honolulu and Cape Cod. But they also include places like Shreveport, Louisiana, and Pittsfield, Massachusetts. For these places that are not tourist destinations, the economic and social future is troubling to contemplate.

PLUG-AND-PLAY COMMUNITIES

Why do some places become destinations for the creative while others don't? Economists speak of the importance of industries having "low entry barriers," so that new firms can easily enter and keep the industry vital. Similarly, I think it's important for a place to have low entry barriers for people—that is, to be a place where newcomers are accepted quickly into all sorts of social and economic arrangements. All else being equal, they are likely to attract greater numbers of talented and creative people—the sort of people who power innovation and growth. Places that thrive in today's world tend to be plug-and-play communities where anyone can fit in quickly. These are places where people can find opportunity, build support structures, be themselves, and not get stuck in any one identity. The plug-and-play community is one that somebody can move into and put together a life—or at least the facsimile of a life—in a week.

Creative centers also tend to be places with thick labor markets that can fulfill the employment needs of members of the creative class, who, by and large, are not looking just for "a job" but for places that offer many employment opportunities.

Cities and regions that attract lots of creative talent are also those with greater diversity and higher levels of quality of place. That's because location choices of the creative class are based to a large degree on their lifestyle interests, and these go well beyond the standard "quality-of-life" amenities that most experts think are important.

For instance, in 1998, I met Gary Gates, then a doctoral student at Carnegie Mellon. While I had been studying the location choices of high-tech industries and talented people, Gates had been exploring the location patterns of gay people. My list of the country's high-tech hot spots looked an awful lot like his list of the places with highest concentrations of gay people. When we compared these two lists with more statistical rigor, his Gay

Index turned out to correlate very strongly to my own measures of high-tech growth. Other measures I came up with, like the Bohemian Index—a measure of artists, writers, and performers— produced similar results.

Talented people seek an environment open to differences. Many highly creative people, regardless of ethnic background or sexual orientation, grew up feeling like outsiders, different in some way from most of their schoolmates. When they are sizing up a new company and community, acceptance of diversity and of gays in particular is a sign that reads "Nonstandard People Welcome Here."

The creative-class people I study use the word *diversity* a lot, but not to press any political hot buttons. Diversity is simply something they value in all its manifestations. This is spoken of so often, and so matter-of-factly, that I take it to be a fundamental marker of creative-class values. Creative-minded people enjoy a mix of influences. They want to hear different kinds of music and try different kinds of food. They want to meet and socialize with people unlike themselves, trade views, and spar over issues.

As with employers, visible diversity serves as a signal that a community embraces the open meritocratic values of the creative age. The people I talked to also desired nightlife with a wide mix of options. The most highly valued options were experiential ones—interesting music venues, neighborhood art galleries, performance spaces, and theaters. A vibrant, varied nightlife was viewed by many as another signal that a city "gets it," even by those who infrequently partake in nightlife. More than anything, the creative class craves real experiences in the real world.

They favor active, participatory recreation over passive, institutionalized forms. They prefer indigenous street-level culture—

a teeming blend of cafés, sidewalk musicians, and small galleries and bistros, where it is hard to draw the line between performers and spectators. They crave stimulation, not escape. They want to pack their time full of dense, high-quality, multidimensional experiences. Seldom has one of my subjects expressed a desire to get away from it all. They want to get into it all, and do it with eyes wide open.

Creative-class people value active outdoor recreation very highly. They are drawn to places and communities where many outdoor activities are prevalent—both because they enjoy these activities and because their presence is seen as a signal that the place is amenable to the broader creative lifestyle. The creative-class people in my studies are into a variety of active sports, from traditional ones like bicycling, jogging, and kayaking to newer, more extreme ones, like trail running and snowboarding.

Places are also valued for authenticity and uniqueness. Authenticity comes from several aspects of a community—historic buildings, established neighborhoods, a unique music scene, or specific cultural attributes. It comes from the mix—from urban grit alongside renovated buildings, from the commingling of young and old, longtime neighborhood characters and yuppies, fashion models and "bag ladies." An authentic place also offers unique and original experiences. Thus a place full of chain stores, chain restaurants, and nightclubs is not authentic. You could have the same experience anywhere.

Today, it seems, leading creative centers provide a solid mix of high-tech industry, plentiful outdoor amenities, and an older urban center whose rebirth has been fueled in part by a combination of creativity and innovative technology, as well as lifestyle amenities. These include places like the greater Boston area,

Small-Size Cities Creativity Rankings

Rankings of 63 metro areas reporting populations
250,000 to 500,000 in the 2000 Census

TOP TEN CITIES

City	Creativity Index	% Creative Workers	Creative Rank	High-Tech Rank	Innovation Rank	Diversity Rank
1. Madison, WI	925	32.8	6	16	4	9
2. Des Moines, IA	862	32.1	8	2	16	20
3. Santa Barbara, CA	856	28.3	19	8	8	7
4. Melbourne, FL	855	35.5	1	6	9	32
5. Boise City, ID	854	35.2	3	1	1	46
6. Huntsville, AL	799	35.3	2	5	18	40
7. Lansing, MI	739	34.3	4	27	29	18
8. Binghamton, NY	731	30.8	12	7	3	60
9. Lexington, KY	717	27.0	28	24	10	12
10. New London, CT	715	28.1	23	11	13	33

BOTTOM TEN CITIES

City	Creativity Index	% Creative Workers	Creative Rank	High-Tech Rank	Innovation Rank	Diversity Rank
63. Shreveport, LA	233	22.1	55	32	59	57
62. Ocala, FL	263	16.4	63	61	52	24
61. Visalia, CA	289	22.9	52	63	60	11
60. Killeen, TX	302	24.6	47	47	51	53
59. Fayetteville, NC	309	29.0	16	62	62	49
58. York, PA	360	22.3	54	54	26	52
57. Fayetteville, AR	366	21.1	57	57	42	17
56. Beaumont, TX	372	27.8	25	37	56	55
55. Lakeland, FL	385	20.9	59	56	53	5
54. Hickory, NC	393	19.4	61	48	32	30

which has the Route 128 suburban complex, Harvard and MIT, and several charming inner-city Boston neighborhoods. Seattle has suburban Bellevue and Redmond (where Microsoft is located), beautiful mountains and country, and a series of revitalized urban neighborhoods. The San Francisco Bay area has everything from posh inner-city neighborhoods to ultrahip districts like SoMa (South of Market) and lifestyle enclaves like Marin County as well as the Silicon Valley. Even Austin includes traditional high-tech developments to the north, lifestyle centers for cycling and outdoor activities, and a revitalizing university/downtown community centered on vibrant Sixth Street, the warehouse district, and the music scene—a critical element of a thriving creative center.

INSTITUTIONAL SCLEROSIS

Even as places like Austin and Seattle are thriving, much of the country is failing to adapt to the demands of the creative age. It is not that struggling cities like Pittsburgh do not want to grow or encourage high-tech industries. In most cases, their leaders are doing everything they think they can to spur innovation and high-tech growth. But most of the time they are either unwilling or unable to do the things required to create an environment or habitat attractive to the creative class. They pay lip service to the need to "attract talent," but continue to pour resources into recruiting call centers, underwriting big-box retailers, subsidizing downtown malls, and squandering precious taxpayer dollars on extravagant stadium complexes. Or they try to create facsimiles of neighborhoods or retail districts, replacing the old and authentic with the new and generic—and in doing so drive the creative class away.

It is a telling commentary on our age that at a time when political will seems difficult to muster for virtually anything, city after city can generate the political capital to underwrite hundreds of millions of dollars of investments in professional sports stadiums. And you know what? They don't matter to the creative class. Not once during any of my focus groups and interviews did the members of the creative class mention professional sports as playing a role of any sort in their choice of where to live and work. What makes most cities unable to even imagine devoting those kinds of resources or political will to do the things that people say really matter to them?

The answer is simple. These cities are trapped by their past. Despite the lip service they might pay, they are unwilling or unable to do what it takes to attract the creative class. The late economist Mancur Olson long ago noted that the decline of nations and regions is a product of an organizational and cultural hardening of the arteries he called "institutional sclerosis." Places that grow up and prosper in one era, Olson argued, find it difficult and oftentimes impossible to adopt new organizational and cultural patterns, regardless of how beneficial they might be. Consequently, innovation and growth shift to new places, which can adapt to and harness these shifts for their benefit. This phenomenon, he contends, is how England got trapped and how the United States became the world's great economic power. It also accounts for the shift in economic activity from the old industrial cities to newer cities in the South and West, according to Olson.

Olson's analysis presciently identifies why so many cities across the nation remain trapped in the culture and attitudes of the by-gone organizational age, unable or unwilling to adapt to current trends. Cities like Detroit, Cleveland, and my current hometown of Pittsburgh were at the forefront of the organizational age. The cultural and attitudinal norms of that age became so powerfully ingrained in these places that they did not allow the new norms and attitudes associated with the creative age to grow up, diffuse, and become generally accepted. This process, in turn, stamped out much of the creative impulse, causing talented and creative people to seek out new places where they could more readily plug in and make a go of it.

Most experts and scholars have not even begun to think in terms of a creative community. Instead, they tend to try to emu-late the Silicon Valley model that author Joel Kotkin has dubbed the "nerdistan." But the nerdistan is a limited economic develop-ment model, which misunderstands the role played by creativity in generating innovation and economic growth. Nerdistans are bland, uninteresting places with acre upon acre of identical of-fice complexes, row after row of asphalt parking lots, freeways clogged with cars, cookie-cutter housing developments, and strip malls sprawling in every direction. Many of these places have fallen victim to the very kinds of problems they were supposed to avoid. The comfort and security of places like Silicon Valley have gradually given way to sprawl, pollution, and paralyzing traffic jams. As one technology executive told the *Wall Street Journal,* "I really didn't want to live in San Jose. Every time I went up there, the concrete jungle got me down." His company eventually set-tled on a more urban Southern California location in downtown Pasadena close to the Caltech campus.

Kotkin finds that the lack of lifestyle amenities is causing sig-

THE RISE OF THE CREATIVE CLASS   83

nificant problems in attracting top creative people to places like
the North Carolina Research Triangle. He quotes a major real
estate developer as saying, "Ask anyone where downtown is and
nobody can tell you. There's not much of a sense of place here . . .
The people I am selling space to are screaming about cultural issues." The Research Triangle lacks the hip urban lifestyle found
in places like San Francisco, Seattle, New York, and Chicago,
laments a University of North Carolina researcher: "In Raleigh-
Durham, we can always visit the hog farms."

THE KIDS ARE ALL RIGHT

How do you build a truly creative community—one that can survive and prosper in this emerging age? The key can no longer be
found in the usual strategies. Recruiting more companies won't
do it; neither will trying to become the next Silicon Valley. While
it certainly remains important to have a solid business climate,
having an effective people climate is even more essential. By
this I mean a general strategy aimed at attracting and retaining
people—especially, but not limited to, creative people. This entails remaining open to diversity and actively working to cultivate
it, and investing in the lifestyle amenities that people really want
and use often, as opposed to using financial incentives to attract
companies, build professional sports stadiums, or develop retail
complexes.

The benefits of this kind of strategy are obvious. Whereas
companies—or sports teams, for that matter—that get financial
incentives can pull up and leave at virtually a moment's notice,

investments in amenities like urban parks, for example, last for generations. Other amenities—like bike lanes or off-road trails for running, cycling, Rollerblading, or just walking your dog—benefit a wide swath of the population.

There is no one-size-fits-all model for a successful people climate. The members of the creative class are diverse across the dimensions of age, ethnicity and race, marital status, and sexual preference. An effective people climate needs to emphasize openness and diversity, and to help reinforce low barriers to entry. Thus it cannot be restrictive or monolithic.

Openness to immigration is particularly important for smaller cities and regions, while the ability to attract so-called bohemians is key for larger cities and regions. For cities and regions to attract these groups, they need to develop the kinds of people climates that appeal to them and meet their needs.

Yet if you ask most community leaders what kinds of people they'd most want to attract, they'd likely say successful married couples in their thirties and forties—people with good middle- to upper-income jobs and stable family lives. I certainly think it is important for cities and communities to be good for children and families. But less than a quarter of all American households consist of traditional nuclear families, and focusing solely on their needs has been a losing strategy, one that neglects a critical engine of economic growth: young people.

Young workers have typically been thought of as transients who contribute little to a city's bottom line. But in the creative age, they matter for two reasons. First, they are workhorses. They are able to work longer and harder, and are more prone to take risks, precisely because they are young and childless. In rapidly changing industries, it's often the most recent graduates who have the most up-to-date skills. Second, people are staying single longer. The average age of marriage for both men and women has risen some five years over the past generation. College-educated people postpone marriage longer than the national averages. Among this group, one of the fastest-growing categories is the never-been-married. To prosper in the creative age, regions have to offer a people climate that satisfies this group's social interests and lifestyle needs, as well as address those of other groups.

Furthermore, a climate oriented to young people is also attractive to the creative class more broadly. Creative-class people do not lose their lifestyle preferences as they age. They don't stop bicycling or running, for instance, just because they have children. When they put their children in child seats or jogging strollers, amenities like traffic-free bike paths become more important than ever. They also continue to value diversity and tolerance. The middle-aged and older people I speak with may no longer hang around in nightspots until 4 A.M., but they enjoy stimulating, dynamic places with high levels of cultural interplay. And if they have children, that's the kind of environment in which they want them to grow up.

My adopted hometown of Pittsburgh has been slow to realize this. City leaders continue to promote Pittsburgh as a place that is good for families, seemingly unaware of the demographic changes that have made young people, singles, new immigrants, and gays critical to the emerging social fabric. People in focus groups I have conducted feel that Pittsburgh is not open to minority groups, new immigrants, or gays. Young women feel there are substantial barriers to their advancement. Talented members of racial and ethnic minorities, as well as professional women, express their desire to leave the city at a rate far greater than their white male counterparts. So do creative people from all walks of life.

Is there hope for Pittsburgh? Of course there is. First, although the region's economy is not dynamic, neither is it the basket case it could easily have become. Twenty years ago there were no significant venture capital firms in the area; now there are many, and thriving high-tech firms continue to form and make their mark. There are signs of life in the social and cultural milieu as well. The region's immigrant population has begun to tick upward, fed by students and professors at the universities and employees in the medical and technology sectors. Major suburbs to the east of the city now have Hindu temples and a growing Indian American population. The area's gay community, while not large, has become more active and visible. Pittsburgh's increasing status in the gay world is reflected in the fact that it is the "location" for Showtime's *Queer as Folk* series.

Many of Pittsburgh's creative class have proven to be relentless cultural builders. The Andy Warhol Museum and the Mattress Factory, a museum/workspace devoted to large-scale installation art, have achieved worldwide recognition. Street-level culture has a growing foothold in Pittsburgh, too, as main street corridors in several older working-class districts have been transformed. Political leaders are in some cases open to new models of development. Pittsburgh mayor Tom Murphy has been an ardent promoter of biking and foot trails, among other things. The city contains absolutely first-rate architecture and its urban design community has become much more vocal about the need to preserve historic buildings, invest in neighborhoods, and institute tough design standards. It would be very hard today (dare I say nearly impossible) to knock down historic buildings and dismember vibrant urban neighborhoods as was done in the past. As these new groups and efforts reach critical mass, the norms and attitudes that have long prevailed in the city are being challenged.

For what it's worth, I'll put my money—and a lot of my effort—into Pittsburgh's making it. If Pittsburgh, with all of its assets and its emerging human creativity, somehow can't make it in the creative age, I fear the future does not bode well for other older industrial communities and established cities, and the lamentable new class segregation among cities will continue to worsen.

The Rules of Innovation

CLAYTON M. CHRISTENSEN

Two decades ago, when I was just out of graduate school and working in the automotive industry, I got my first introduction to the statistical process-control chart. We used this laborious technique to make sure the machines employed in our manufacturing process did not drift out of control. Composed of three parallel horizontal lines, the "SPC" chart has long been an important tool in quality management. The center line represents the targeted value for the critical performance parameter of a product being manufactured. The lines above and below it represent the acceptable upper and lower control limits. If the product were, say, an axle, workers would plot the thickness of each piece they made on the chart. When I asked why there was typically a scatter of points around the target, my managers cited the randomness inherent in all processes.

The "Quality Movement" of the 1980s and '90s subsequently taught us that there isn't randomness in processes. Every deviation of the actual value from the target has a cause. It appears to be random when we don't know the cause. The Quality Movement developed methods for identifying those additional factors—and we discovered that if we could control or account for all of them, the result would be perfectly predictable, and there would be no need to inspect products as they emerged from manufacturing. The management of innovation today is where the Quality Movement was twenty years ago, in that many believe the outcomes of innovation efforts are unpredictable. The raison d'être of the venture capital industry is belief in the unpredictability of new businesses. A few ventures will succeed; most won't, the VCs say. They therefore place a portfolio of bets, extracting premium prices for their capital in order to earn the high return required to compensate for the risk that unpredictability imposes. I believe, however, that innovation *isn't* random. Every undesired outcome has a cause. Those outcomes *appear* to be random when we don't understand all the factors that affect successful innovation. If we could understand and manage these variables, innovation wouldn't be nearly as risky as it appears.

The good news is that recent years have seen considerable progress in identifying important variables that affect the probability of success in innovation. I've classified these variables into four sets: (1) taking root in disruption, (2) the necessary scope to succeed, (3) leveraging the right capabilities, and (4) disrupting competitors, not customers.

Of course, building successful businesses is such a complicated process, involving subtle interdependencies among so many variables in dynamic systems, that we're unlikely ever to make it perfectly predictable. But the more we can master these variables, the more we will be able to create new companies, products, processes, and services that achieve what we hope to achieve.

TAKE ROOT IN DISRUPTION

The startling conclusion suggested by the research that led to my writing *The Innovator's Dilemma* was that many successful companies stumble from prominence not because they're badly managed but precisely because they are *well managed*. They listen to and satisfy the needs of their best customers, and they focus investments at the largest and most profitable tiers of their markets. Mastering these paradigms of good management gives established companies, as a group, an extraordinary track record in producing *sustaining* innovations that bring better products to established markets. It matters little whether the innovation is incrementally simple or radically difficult, as long as it enables good companies to make better products that they can sell for higher margins to their best customers in attractively sized markets. The companies that had led their industries in prior technologies led their industries in adopting new sustaining technologies in literally *100 percent* of the cases we studied.

In contrast, the leading companies almost always were toppled when *disruptive* technologies emerged—products or services that weren't as good as those already used in established markets. Disruptive innovations don't initially perform well enough to be sold or used successfully in mainstream markets. But they have other attributes—most often simplicity, convenience, and low cost—that appeal to a new, small, and initially unattractive (to established firms) set of customers, who use them in new or low-end applications. The chances that a new company could become successful if its entry path was a *sustaining* strategy—trying to make a better product than the incumbents and selling it to the same customers—were about 6 percent in our study. The chances of success for firms that entered with a disruptive strategy were 33 percent. The disparity stems from the motivation and position of the leading firms. They have far more resources to throw at opportunities than entrants do. When newcomers attack customers and markets attractive to the leaders, the leaders overwhelm them.

All companies are burdened with "asymmetric" motivations in that they must move toward markets that promise higher profit margins and the most substantial and immediate growth and cannot move down market toward smaller opportunities and profit margins. When new entrants take root with customers in markets that are unattractive to the leaders, they are safer—and it has nothing to do with how much cash or proprietary technology they have. They are safe because the incumbents are motivated to ignore or even exit the very markets that the entrants are motivated to enter. Taking root in disruption, therefore, is the first condition that innovators need to meet to improve the probability of successfully creating a new growth business. If they cannot or do not do this, their odds of success are much smaller.

There are two tests to assess whether a market can be disrupted. At least one of these criteria must be met in order for an upstart to be disruptively successful. If a new growth business can meet both, the odds are even better.

1. Does the innovation enable less skilled or less wealthy customers to do for themselves things that only the wealthy or skilled intermediaries could previously do?

When an innovation fulfills this condition, even if it can't do all the things existing offerings can, potential customers excluded from the market tend to be delighted. For example, many people loved the first personal computers, no matter how clunky the booting process and limited the software the machines could run, because the alternative to which they compared the PC wasn't the minicomputer—it was no computer at all. Filling such a void reduces the capital commitments and technological achievements required for an innovation to become viable and creates new growth markets. I call the process of finding and nurturing these opportunities "creative creation." After a technology takes root in new markets, and after new growth is created, disruption can invade the established market and destroy its leading firms.

Even if innovators succeed in cramming disruptive technology into an existing market application, the incumbents typically win. Digital photography, online consumer banking, and hybrid-electric vehicles are examples of potentially disruptive technologies that were deployed in such a sustaining fashion. Billions were spent on these innovations to beat out already acceptable and habitual technology; little net growth resulted, as sales of the new products cannibalized sales of the old; and the industry leaders maintained their rule.

2. Does the innovation target customers at the low end of a market who don't need all the functionality of current products? And does the business model enable the disruptive innovator to earn attractive returns at discount prices unattractive to the incumbents?

Wal-Mart, Dell Computer, and Nucor are examples of disruptive companies that attacked the low ends of their markets with business models that allowed them to make money at discount prices. Wal-Mart started by selling brand-name products at prices 20 percent below department-store prices and still earned attractive returns because it turned inventory over much more frequently. Such a disruptive strategy can create new growth businesses but does not create new markets or classes of consumers. It has a high probability of success because the reported profit margins of established companies typically improve if they get out of low-end, low-margin products and add in their stead high-margin products positioned in more demanding market segments. By assaulting the low end of the market and then moving up, a new company attacks, tier by tier, the markets from which established competitors are motivated to exit.

PICK THE SCOPE NEEDED TO SUCCEED

The second set of variables that affects the probability that a new business venture will succeed relates to its degree of "integration." Highly integrated companies make and sell their own proprietary components and products across a wide range of product lines or businesses. Nonintegrated companies outsource as much as possible to suppliers and partners and use modular, open systems and components. Which style is likely to be successful is determined by the conditions under which companies must compete as disruption occurs.

In markets where product functionality is not yet good enough, companies must compete by making better products. This typically means making products whose architecture is interdependent and proprietary, because competitive pressure compels engineers to fit the pieces of their systems together in ever more efficient ways in order to wring the best performance possible out of the available technology. Standardization of interfaces (meaning fewer degrees of design freedom) forces them to back away from the frontier of what is technologically possible—which spells competitive trouble when functionality is inadequate. This helps explain why IBM, General Motors, Apple Computer, RCA, Xerox, and AT&T, as the most integrated firms during the not-good-enough era of their industries' histories, became dominant competitors. Intel and Microsoft (raps about the latter's supposed lack of innovation aside) have also dominated their pieces of the computer industry—compared to less integrated companies such as WordPerfect (now owned by Corel)—because their products have employed the sorts of proprietary, interdependent architectures that are necessary when pushing the frontier of what is possible. This also helps us understand why NTT DoCoMo, with its integrated strategy, has been so much more successful in providing mobile access to the Internet than nonintegrated American and European competitors who have sought to interface with one another through negotiated standards. When the functionality of products has overshot what mainstream customers can use, however, companies must compete through improvements in speed to market, simplicity and convenience, and the ability to customize products to the needs of customers in ever smaller market niches. Here, competitive forces drive the design of *modular* products, in which the interfaces among components and subsystems are clearly specified. Ultimately, these coalesce as industry standards. Modular architectures help companies respond to individual customer needs and introduce new products faster by upgrading individual subsystems without having to redesign everything. Under these conditions (and only under these conditions), outsourcing titans like Dell and Cisco Systems can prosper—because modular architectures help them be fast, flexible and responsive.

LEVERAGE THE RIGHT CAPABILITIES

Innovations fail when managers attempt to implement them within organizations that are incapable of succeeding. Managers can determine the innovation limits of their organizations quite precisely by asking three questions: (1) Do I have the resources to succeed? (2) Will my organization's processes facilitate success in this new effort? (3) Will my organization's values allow employees to prioritize this innovation, given their other responsibilities?

Beyond technology, the resources that drive innovative success are managers and money. Corporate executives often tap managers who have strong records of success in the mainstream to manage the creation of new growth businesses. Such choices can be the kiss of death, however, because the challenges confronting managers in a disruptive enterprise—and the skills required to overcome them—are different from those that prevail in the core business. Many innovations fail because managers do not know what they do not know as they make and implement their plans. That is, they assume that the same strategies and customer needs that apply in mature, stable markets will apply in disruptive ventures. But this is not the case, and by making such assumptions, managers close themselves off from opportunities to discover what customers really find useful in new, disruptive products. Innovators must avoid two common misconceptions in managing the other key resource, money. The first is that deep corporate pockets are an advantage when growing new businesses. They are not. Too much cash allows those running a new venture to follow a flawed strategy for too long. Having barely enough money forces the venture's managers to adapt to the desires of actual customers, rather than those of the corporate treasury, when looking for ways to get money—and forces them to uncover a viable strategy more quickly.

The second misconception is that patience is a virtue—that innovation entails large losses for sustained periods prior to reaping the huge upside that comes from disruptive technologies. Innovators should *be patient about the new venture's size but impatient for profits.* The mandate to be profitable forces the venture to zero in on a valid strategy. But when new ventures are forced to get big fast, they end up placing huge bets at a time when the right strategy simply cannot be known. In particular, they tend to target large, obvious, existing markets—and this condemns them to failure. Most of today's envisioned business opportunities for wireless Internet access, for example, involve big applications such as stock trading and multiplayer gaming that have already found homes on wired, desktop computers. Billions are being sunk into new wireless ventures committed to taking over these markets before innovators have a chance to learn what applications wireless is really best at delivering.

Resources such as technology, cash, and technical talent tend to be flexible, in that they can be used for a wide array of purposes. Processes, however—the central element in our second question—are typically inflexible. Their purpose is not to adapt quickly but to get the same job done reliably, again and again. The fact that a process facilitates certain tasks means that it will not work well for very different tasks. Failure is frequently rooted in the forced use of habitual but inappropriate processes for doing market research, strategic planning, and budgeting.

Sony, for example, was history's most successful disruptor. Between 1950 and 1980, it introduced twelve bona fide disruptive technologies that created exciting new markets and ultimately dethroned industry leaders—everything from radios and televisions to VCRs and the Walkman. Between 1980 and 1997, however, the company did not introduce a single disruptive innovation. Sony continued to produce sustaining innovations in its product businesses, of course. But even the new businesses that it created with its PlayStation and Vaio notebook computer were great but late entries into already established markets.

What drove Sony's shift from a disruptive to a sustaining innovation strategy? Prior to 1980, all new product launch decisions were made by cofounder Akio Morita and a trusted team of associates. They never did market research, believing that if markets did not exist they could not be analyzed. Their process for assessing new opportunities relied on personal intuition. In the 1980s, Morita withdrew from active management in order to be more involved in Japanese politics. The company consequently began hiring marketing and product-planning professionals who brought with them data-intensive, analytical processes of doing market research. Those processes were very good at uncovering unmet customer needs in existing product markets. But making the intuitive bets required to launch disruptive businesses became impossible.

A company's values—the focus of question three—determine the necessity of spinning out separate organizations for new ventures. Values are even less flexible than resources. *Everyone* in an organization—executives to sales force—must put a premium on the type of business that helps the company make money given its existing cost structure. If a new venture doesn't target order sizes, price points, and margins that are more attractive than other opportunities on the organization's plate, it won't get priority resources; it will languish and ultimately fail.

Nor is it just the values of the innovating company that matter, because suppliers and distributors have values, too, and *they* must put the highest priorities on opportunities that help *them* make money. This is why, with almost no exceptions, disruptive innovations take root in freestanding value networks—with new sales forces, distributors, and retailing channels.

DISRUPT COMPETITORS, NOT CUSTOMERS

The fourth factor in successful innovation is minimizing the need for customers to reorder their lives. If an innovation helps customers do things they are already trying to do more simply and conveniently, it has a higher probability of success. If it makes it easier for customers to do something they weren't trying to do anyway, it will fail. Put differently, innovators should try to disrupt their competitors, never their customers.

The best way to understand what customers are actually trying to do, as opposed to what they say they want to do, is to *watch* them. For example, when interviewed by the college textbook industry, students say they would welcome the ability to probe more deeply into topics of interest that textbooks just touch on. In response, publishers have invested substantial sums to make richer information available on CDs and Web sites. But few students actually use these innovations, and little growth has resulted. Why? Because what most students *really* are trying to do is avoid reading textbooks at all. They say they would like to delve more deeply into their subjects. But what they really *do* is put off reading until the last possible minute—and then cram. To make it simpler and more convenient for students to do what they already are trying to do, a publisher could create an online facility called Cramming. Like all disruptive technologies, it would take root in a low-end market: the least conscientious students. Semester after semester, Cramming would then improve as a new "cramming-aid" growth business, without affecting textbook sales. Conscientious students would continue to purchase textbooks. At some point, however, learning the material online would be so much easier and less expensive that, tier by tier, students would stop buying texts. This path of innovation has a much higher chance of success than a direct assault that pits digital texts against conventional textbooks.

The observed probabilities of success in innovation are low. But these statistics stem from the sum of sustaining and disruptive strategies, many of which are attempted in organizations whose resources, processes, and values render them incapable of succeeding. Many innovators draw lessons from observing other successful companies in very different circumstances and attempt to succeed with just one or a few links in a chain of interdependent values. And many fail after assuming that what customers say they want to do is what they actually *would* do.

Hence, the observed probabilities of success don't necessarily reflect what the true likelihood of success can be, if the critical variables in the complex and dynamic process of innovation are understood and managed effectively. Indeed, success may not be as difficult to achieve as it has seemed.

Customers as Innovators

A New Way to Create Value

STEFAN THOMKE AND ERIC VON HIPPEL

L isten carefully to what your customers want and then respond
with new products that meet or exceed their needs." That man-
tra has dominated many a business, and it has undoubtedly led to
great products and has even shaped entire industries. But slav-
ishly obeying that conventional wisdom can also threaten a company's ability to compete.

The difficulty is that fully understanding customers' needs is
often a costly and inexact process. Even when customers know
precisely what they want, they often cannot transfer that information to manufacturers clearly or completely. Today, as the pace
of change in many markets accelerates and as some industries
move toward serving "markets of one," the cost of understanding and responding to customers' needs can easily spiral out of
control.

In the course of studying product innovation across many

industries, we have discovered that a number of companies have adopted an intriguing approach, which at first seems counterintuitive. Essentially, these companies have abandoned their efforts to understand exactly what products their customers want and have instead equipped them with tools to design and develop their own products, ranging from minor modifications to major new innovations. The user-friendly tools, often integrated into a package we call a "tool kit for customer innovation," deploy new technologies like computer simulation and rapid prototyping to make product development faster and less expensive.[1]

A variety of industries use this approach. Bush Boake Allen (BBA), a global supplier of specialty flavors to companies like Nestlé, has built a tool kit that enables its customers to develop their own flavors, which BBA then manufactures. In the materials field, GE provides customers with Web-based tools for designing better plastic products. In software, a number of companies let people add custom-designed modules to their standard products and then commercialize the best of those components. Open-source software allows users to design, build, distribute, and support their own programs—no manufacturer required. Indeed, the trend toward customers as innovators has the power to completely transform industries. In the semiconductor business, it has led to a custom chip market that has grown to more than $15 billion.

Tapping into customer innovation can certainly generate tremendous value, but capturing that value is hardly a simple or straightforward process. Not only must companies develop the right tool kit, they must also revamp their business models as well as their management mind-sets. When companies relinquish a fundamental task—such as designing a new product—to customers, the two parties must redefine their relationship, and this change can be risky. With custom computer chips, for instance, companies traditionally captured value by both designing and manufacturing innovative products. Now, with customers taking over more of the design task, companies must focus more intently on providing the best custom manufacturing. In other words, the location where value is both created and captured changes, and companies must reconfigure their business models accordingly. In this article, we offer some basic principles and lessons for industries undergoing such a transformation.

A COSTLY PROBLEM—AND A RADICAL SOLUTION

In a nutshell, product development is often difficult because the "need" information (what the customer wants) resides with the customer, and the "solution" information (how to satisfy those needs) lies with the manufacturer. Traditionally, the onus has been on manufacturers to collect the need information through various means, including market research and information gathered from the field. The process can be costly and time-consuming because customer needs are often complex, subtle, and fast changing. Frequently, customers don't fully understand their needs until they try out prototypes to explore exactly what does, and doesn't, work (referred to as "learning by doing").

Not surprisingly, traditional product development is a drawn-out process of trial and error, often ping-ponging between manufacturer and customer. First, the manufacturer develops a prototype based on information from customers that is incomplete and only partially correct. The customer then tries out the product, finds flaws, and requests corrections. The cycle repeats until a satisfactory solution is reached, often requiring many costly and time-consuming iterations.

To appreciate the extent of the difficulty, consider product development at BBA (now International Flavors and Fragrances). In this industry, specialty flavors are created to bolster and enhance the taste of nearly all processed foods because manufacturing techniques weaken the real flavors. The development of those added flavors requires a high degree of customization and expertise, and the practice remains more an art than a science.

A traditional product development project at BBA might progress in the following way: A customer requests a meaty flavor for a soy product, and the sample must be delivered within a week. BBA marketing professionals and flavorists jump into action, and the sample is shipped in six days. A frustrating three weeks ensue until the client responds with, "It's good, but we need it less smoky and more gutsy." The client knows precisely what that means, but BBA flavorists find the request difficult to interpret. The result is more frenzied activity as BBA struggles to adjust the flavor in a couple days. Depending on the product, BBA and the client could go back and forth for several more iterations. This represents a huge problem because clients often expect BBA to get the flavor right the first time, or within two or three iterations.

To make matters worse, BBA bears most of the development risk. The company collects revenue only after both the client and consumers are fully satisfied. R&D expenses could be just $1,000 for tweaking an existing flavor, but they could go as high as $300,000 for an entirely new family of flavors that require not only chemists and flavorists but also sales, marketing, regulatory, and quality control expertise. On average, the client eventually accepts only 15 percent of all new flavors for full market evaluation, and only 5 percent to 10 percent make their way to the marketplace. Meanwhile, margins in the flavor industry have been falling because of increased competition and cost pressures from customers.

In response, BBA's CEO Julian Boyden and VP of Technology John Wright investigated the option of shifting more innovation activities to customers. The company developed an Internet-based tool containing a large database of flavor profiles. A customer can select and manipulate that information on a computer screen and send his new design directly to an automated machine (perhaps located at the customer site) that will manufacture a sample within minutes. After tasting the sample, the customer can make any adjustments that are needed. If the flavor is too salty, for instance, he can easily tweak that parameter on the profile and have the machine immediately produce another sample.

It is important to note that outsourcing product development to customers does not eliminate learning by doing—nor should it. What it does is make traditional product development better and faster—for two reasons. First, a company can bypass the expensive and error-prone effort to understand customer needs in detail. Second, the trial-and-error cycles that inevitably occur during product development can progress much more quickly because the iterations will be performed solely by the customer. (For a basic illustration of the customers-as-innovators approach, see the exhibit "A New Approach to Developing Custom Products.")

But developing the right tool kit for customers is hardly a

A New Approach to Developing Custom Products

Traditionally, suppliers have taken on most of the work—and responsibility—of product development. The result has been costly and time-consuming iterations between supplier and customer to reach a satisfactory solution. With the customers-as-innovators approach, a supplier provides customers with tools so that they can design and develop the application-specific part of a product on their own. This shifts the location of the supplier-customer interface, and the trial-and-error iterations necessary for product development are now carried out by the customer only. The result is greatly increased speed and effectiveness.

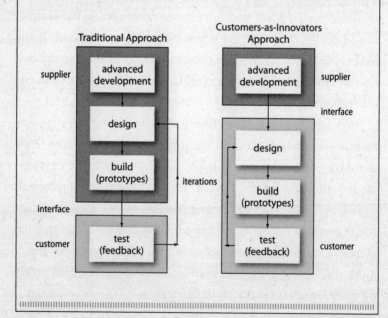

When Customer Innovation Makes Sense

From our research, we have identified three major signs that your industry may soon migrate to a customers-as-innovators approach:

1. Your market segments are shrinking, and customers are increasingly asking for customized products. As you try to respond to those demands, your costs increase, and it is difficult to pass those costs on to customers.

2. You and your customers need many iterations before you find a solution. Some customers complain that you have gotten the product wrong or that you are responding too slowly. You are tempted to restrict the degree to which your products can be customized, and your smaller customers must make do with standard products or find a better solution elsewhere. As a result, customer loyalty starts to erode.

3. You or your competitors use high-quality computer-based simulation and rapid-prototyping tools internally to develop new products. You also have computer-adjustable production processes that can manufacture custom products. (These technologies could form the foundation of a tool kit that customers could use to develop their own designs.)

---

simple matter.[2] Specifically, tool kits must provide four important capabilities. First and most important, they must enable people to complete a series of design cycles followed by learning by doing. Computer simulation, for example, allows customers to quickly try out ideas and design alternatives without having to manufacture the actual products. When the simulation technology lacks the desired accuracy, it can be supplemented with rapid prototyping methods. Second, tool kits must be user-friendly. They should not require customers to learn an entirely new design language. (Flavorists, for example, think in terms of formulations and chemical compounds, whereas customers think of tastes such as smoky, sweet, fresh, and so on.) Third, they must contain libraries of useful components and modules that have been pretested and debugged. These save customers from having to reinvent the wheel. Instead, people can focus their efforts on the truly novel elements of their design. Fourth, tool kits must contain information about the capabilities and limitations of the production process that will be used to manufacture the product. This will ensure that a customer's design will in fact be producible.

AN INDUSTRY TRANSFORMED

To understand the major impact that the customers-as-innovators approach can have, consider the history of the custom computer chip industry. The story holds several profound lessons about how the right tool kit can turn a market on its ear.

During the late 1970s, suppliers of custom chips experienced the same types of market dynamics that BBA has more recently encountered. (See the sidebar "When Customer Innovation Makes Sense.") At the time a typical user of custom semiconductors, such as a toy manufacturer that needed circuitry to operate its robotic dog, might have hired a chip company to develop a custom design. Because that process was complicated and costly, the chip company could afford to undertake projects only for high-volume customers.

Then a handful of start-ups turned everything upside down. Companies like LSI Logic Corporation and VLSI Technology provided both large and small customers with do-it-yourself tools that enabled them to design their own specialized chips. Customers could benefit by getting what they wanted through their own experimentation, and the fledgling chip companies could profit by manufacturing those customer designs. The win-win solution was right on the money. Between the 1980s and today, the market for such custom-integrated circuits has soared from virtually nothing to more than $15 billion, with the number of customers growing from a handful of high-volume buyers to hundreds of thousands of companies with very diverse end-user applications.

A key to that $15 billion market is the tool-kit technology. In principle, outsourcing custom design to customers can help slash development times and costs, but customers are not experts in a supplier's business. So how could customers be expected to create custom designs that can be produced on a manufacturer's so-phisticated process equipment? The answer to that was found in a major shift that had been taking place in the semiconductor industry.

Traditionally, specialized information used by a manufacturer to design and build custom products has been locked in the minds of the company's development engineers. This knowledge accu-mulates over decades of experience. In recent years, companies have been able to incorporate a considerable amount of this human expertise into computer-based tools. These CAD/CAM programs have grown increasingly sophisticated, and many now contain li-braries of tested and debugged modules that people can simply plug into a new design. The most effective tools also enable rapid testing through computer simulation and provide links to automated equipment that can build prototypes quickly. This leading-edge technology, which manufacturers had been using internally, has become the basic building block for customer tool kits.

When LSI was founded in 1981, R&D engineers at large semiconductor companies were already using many elements of the customer tool kit, but there was no integrated system that less-skilled customers would be comfortable with. So LSI bought some of the pieces, made them customer-friendly by adding graphical user interfaces, and integrated them. The result was a packaged tool kit that let customers design their own chips with little support from LSI.

The brilliant insight that made possible a tool kit for less skilled customers was that the design of the chip's fundamental elements, such as its transistors, could be standardized and could incorporate the manufacturer's solution information of how semiconductors are fabricated. Then all the information the customer needed about how the chip would function could be concentrated within the electrical wiring that connects those fundamental elements. In other words, this new type of chip, called a "gate array," had a novel architecture created specifically to separate the manufacturer's solution information from the customer's need information. As a result, all customers had to do was use a tool kit that could interconnect a gate array based on their specific needs. For its part, LSI had to rethink how to make its production processes more flexible so that it could manufacture the custom chips at low cost.

Customer tool kits based on gate-array technology offer the four major capabilities described earlier. They contain a range of tools, including those to test a design, that enable users to create their own prototypes through trial and error. They are customer-friendly in that they use Boolean algebra, which is the design language commonly taught to electrical engineers. They contain extensive libraries of pretested circuit modules. And they also contain information about production processes so that users can test their designs to ensure that they can be manufactured. Interestingly, more recent technology—chips called field programmable gate arrays (FPGAs)—enable the customer to become both the designer and the manufacturer. Essentially, FPGA tool kits contain design and simulation software and equipment that customers use to program chips for themselves.

THE BENEFITS AND CHALLENGES

Well-designed customer tool kits, such as those developed for the creation of custom semiconductor chips, offer several major advantages over traditional product development. First, they are significantly better at satisfying subtle aspects of customer need because customers know what they need better than manufacturers do. Second, designs will usually be completed much faster because customers can create them at their own site. Third, if customers follow the rules embedded in a tool kit (and if all the technological bugs have been worked out), their designs can be manufactured the first time around.

There are also ancillary benefits. Tool kits enable a company to do business with small customers that might have been prohibitively expensive to work with before, thus expanding the accessible market—and the number of product innovations. By serving these smaller clients, tool kits also reduce the pool of unserved, frustrated potential customers who might turn to competitors or to new entrants into the market. Furthermore, they allow companies to better serve their larger, preferred customers. That's a benefit most suppliers wouldn't expect, because they'd assume that their bigger customers would want the traditional hand-holding to which they're so accustomed. Experience shows, however, that such customers are often willing to use a tool kit, especially when fast product turnaround is crucial.

Of course, tool kits will not satisfy every type of customer. For one thing, they are generally not able to handle every kind of design. Also, they create products that are typically not as technically sophisticated as those developed by experienced engineers at a manufacturer using conventional methods. So manufacturers may continue to design certain products (those with difficult technical demands) while customers take over the design of others (those that require quick turnarounds or a detailed and accurate understanding of the customer's need).

The business challenges of implementing a tool kit can be daunting. Turning customers into innovators requires no less than a radical change in management mind-set. Pioneers LSI Logic and VLSI Technology were successful because they abandoned a principle that had long dominated conventional management thinking at leading companies like IBM, Intel, and Fujitsu. For many years, these companies had assumed that their interests would best be served by keeping design expertise, tools, and technologies away from customers. In contrast, LSI, VLSI, and the other industry upstarts understood that they needed to do just the opposite by putting robust, user-friendly tool kits into customers' hands.

Such a dramatic shift in mind-set required a thorough re-thinking of well-entrenched business practices. In essence, a company that turns its customers into innovators is outsourcing a valuable service that was once proprietary, and the change can be traumatic if that capability has long been a major source of competitive advantage. For example, a common problem is resistance from sales and marketing departments, which have traditionally been responsible for managing relationships with customers and providing first-class service to them. With tool kits, computer-to-computer interactions replace intense person-to-person contact during product development. In other words, customers who design products themselves have little need for a manufacturer's sales or marketing department to determine what they need. If this change affects the compensation of sales representatives in the field, it could easily derail any efforts to alter the company's business model. As a result, senior management needs to face these issues head-on—for example, by determining how the sales and marketing functions should evolve and by using specific incentives to induce employees to support the transformation. (For more on how to adapt your business practices, see the sidebar "Five Steps for Turning Customers into Innovators.")

To better understand these issues, consider GE Plastics, which recently made the bold move of introducing some elements of a Web-based customer tool kit. Doing so required GE Plastics to rethink its sources of competitive advantage and to develop new business models that forced major changes, including the ways in which its sales and marketing staff acquired new customers. The company's story holds several valuable lessons.

GE Plastics does not design or manufacture plastic products but sells resins to those that do, and the properties of those resins must precisely match the properties of both the end product (a cell phone, for instance) as well as the process used to manufacture that product. With the formation of the Polymerland division in 1998, GE Plastics allowed customers to order plastics online and later took the step of making thirty years of its in-house knowledge available on a Web site. Registered users were given access to company data sheets, engineering expertise, and simulation software. Customers could use that knowledge and technology to conduct their own trial-and-error experiments to investigate, for example, how a certain grade of plastic with a specific amount of a particular type of reinforcement would flow into and fill a mold. The approximate cost of bringing such sophisticated tools online: $5 million.

GE Plastics, of course, did not make the investment simply to be magnanimous. Through the Web site, the company identifies and tracks people likely to become customers. That information is then relayed to an e-marketing staff. Today, the Web site attracts about a million visitors per year who are automatically screened for potential sales; that information accounts for nearly one-third of all new customer leads, thus fueling much of GE Plastic's growth. And because the cost of acquiring new business has decreased, GE Plastics can now go after smaller customers it might have ignored in the past. Specifically, the sales threshold at which a potential customer becomes attractive to GE's field marketing has dropped by more than 60 percent.

Five Steps for Turning Customers into Innovators

1. Develop a user-friendly tool kit for customers.

- The tool kit must enable customers to run repeated trial-and-error experiments and tests rapidly and efficiently.
- The technology should let customers work in a familiar design language, making it cheaper for customers to adopt your tool kit.
- The tool kit should include a library of standard design modules so customers can create complex custom designs rapidly.
- The technology should be adapted to your production processes so that customer designs can be sent directly to your manufacturing operations without extensive tailoring.

2. Increase the flexibility of your production processes.

- Your manufacturing operations should be retooled for fast, low-cost production of specialized designs developed by customers.

3. Carefully select the first customers to use the tool kit.

- The best prospects are customers that have a strong need for developing custom products quickly and frequently, have skilled engineers on staff, and have little experience with traditional customization services. These customers will likely stick with you when you are working out the system's bugs.

4. Evolve your tool kit continually and rapidly to satisfy your leading-edge customers.

- Customers at the forefront of technology will always push for improvements in your tool kit. Investments in such advancements will likely pay off, because many of your customers will need tomorrow what leading-edge customers desire today.

continued...

5. Adapt your business practices accordingly.

- Outsourcing product development to customers will require you to revamp your business models to profit from the shift. The change might, for instance, make it economically feasible for you to work with smaller, low-volume customers.
- Tool kits will fundamentally change your relationship with customers. Intense person-to-person contact during product development will, for example, be replaced by computer-to-computer interactions. Prepare for these changes by implementing incentives to reduce resistance from your employees.

The online tools have also enabled GE Plastics to improve customer satisfaction at a lower cost. Before the Web site, GE Plastics received about five hundred thousand customer calls every year. Today, the availability of online tools has slashed that number in half. In fact, customers use the tools more than two thousand times a week. To encourage the rapid adoption of its tool kit, GE Plastics runs about four hundred e-seminars a year that reach roughly eight thousand customers. The company hopes that this effort will help encourage product engineers to design parts made of plastic (and GE resins) when they might otherwise have opted for metal or other materials.

A PATTERN OF MIGRATION

Perhaps the most important lesson to be learned from GE Plastics is that a company that adopts the customers-as-innovators approach must adapt its business accordingly. Furthermore, we've found that because the value that tool kits generate tends to migrate, a company must continually reposition itself to capture that value.

When a supplier introduces a tool kit, the technology first tends to be company specific: the designs can only be produced in the factory of the company that developed the tool kit. This creates a huge short-term advantage for the pioneering supplier, which can reduce its custom design costs because they are partially outsourced to customers. That, in turn, enables the supplier to serve more customers. And because the customer's designs must be produced on the supplier's system, the supplier doesn't risk losing any business.

But the loss of leverage by customers represents a fundamental shift. Traditionally, in the field of specialized industrial products, companies interested in a customer's business develop a custom design and submit it for evaluation. The customer picks the proposal from one supplier, and the others are saddled with a loss for their time and investment. A tool kit tied to a single supplier changes that dynamic: a customer that develops a design using the tool kit cannot ask for competing quotes because only one company can manufacture it.

Of course, customers would prefer the advantages of a tool kit without the associated loss of leverage. In the long run, this type of solution tends to emerge: customer pressure induces third parties to introduce tool kits that can create designs to fit any supplier's manufacturing process. Or, in a slight variation, customers complain until a company that owns a dominant tool kit is forced to allow a spin-off to evolve the technology into a supplier-neutral form. Then customers are free to shop their designs around to competing manufacturers.

In other words, one long-term result of customer tool kits is that manufacturers lose a portion of the value they have traditionally delivered. But if the conditions are ripe for the technology to emerge in a given industry and if customers will benefit from it—and our research shows that they will—then suppliers really don't have a choice. Some company will eventually introduce a tool kit and reap the short-term advantages. Then others must follow. In the case of custom chips, Fujitsu initially resisted making its in-house design technology available to customers, thinking the move was too risky. (See the exhibit "Creating Value with Customers as Innovators.") But after LSI introduced a tool kit and began to establish itself in the market, Fujitsu and others were forced to play catch-up.

QUESTIONS OF VALUE

Predicting where value will migrate—and knowing how to capture it—will be crucial as customer tool kits become more widespread. So far, the customers-as-innovators approach has mainly emerged in the B2B field, but numerous signs indicate that it is also spreading to the B2C arena. Many companies already offer so-called product configurators that enable consumers to obtain a mass-customized version of a standard product. Dell customers, for example, can select various components (a disk drive, monitor, memory modules, and so on) from a menu to assemble the computer best suited to their needs. Eyeglass frames, automobiles, and even Barbie dolls can be similarly configured. In fact, no application seems too trivial. General Mills is planning

Creating Value with Customers as Innovators*

In the electronics market, suppliers have traditionally been the designers of full-custom and application-specific integrated circuits (light gray, with a compound annual growth rate of about 12 percent). During the 1990s, tool kits based on gate-array and standard-cell technologies (medium gray, with a CAGR of about 13 percent) enabled customers and third parties to also become product innovators. With field programmable technology (dark gray, with a CAGR of about 29 percent), customers take on primary responsibility for custom circuit design, creating great value in the industry.

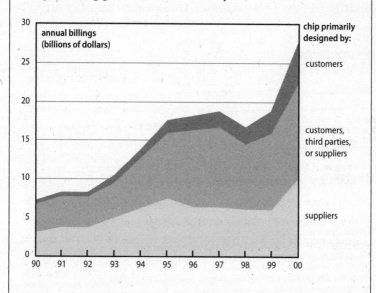

*Figures are from World Semiconductor Trade Statistics for custom metal-oxide semiconductor (MOS) logic, a dominant technology for digital circuits.

to introduce a Web site that will allow consumers to mix and match more than a hundred ingredients to create their own breakfast cereal. Although such product configurators are currently limited in what they can do (for one thing, they don't allow a user to try out a design, either through a prototype or a computer simulation), future versions could approach the functionality of true customer tool kits and allow for radically new innovations. (See the sidebar "What Mass Customization Is—and Isn't.")

Producers of information products, especially software, will perhaps feel the biggest impact. Companies like Microsoft have

What Mass Customization Is—and Isn't

Imagine a mass manufacturer that could customize products for each of its customers. Economically, that would require two things: first, learning how to design specialized products efficiently (the R&D problem), and second, learning how to manufacture those goods cheaply and quickly (the production problem).

The second problem has been addressed by the popular concept of mass-customized production. In that approach, computerized process equipment or flexible assembly procedures can be adjusted quickly and inexpensively so companies can make single-unit quantities of one-of-a-kind products at a cost that is reasonably competitive with the manufacture of similar, mass-produced items. The classic example is Dell Computer: Consumers can buy a Dell computer by picking the major components they want (the size of the hard drive, the kind of monitor, the number and types of memory modules, and so on) from a menu on a Dell Web site. The company assembles and delivers the custom products in days.

But Dell's mass-customization approach does not address the first problem: learning how to design novel custom goods efficiently. The company's customers have only a limited number of standard components and combinations to choose from, leaving them little room for creativity or real innovation. What if someone wants a computer that cannot be assembled from those standard components, or what if that person is uncertain that a particular product will actually fulfill her needs? For instance, will the computer she's assembled be able to run the latest game software without crashing? Unless customers can test a computer design that they've assembled before placing the order, they can't perform the trial-and-error experiments needed to develop the product best suited to their needs. In other words, with mass customization, the cost of manufacturing unique products has dropped, but the cost of designing such items has not.

The approach presented in this article—using tool kits that enable customers to become innovators—targets the first problem; its goal is to provide customers with enough creative freedom to design innovative custom products that will truly satisfy their needs.

long relied on customers to beta-test new products. Now other companies have taken that concept to the next level. Stata, which sells a software package for performing complex statistical analyses, encourages its customers to write software add-on modules for performing the latest statistical techniques; the company then adapts and incorporates the best of those into its next release.

The danger to software companies is that production is essentially free, so the customer might one day mass-distribute copies of a custom program with the simple press of a button. If that practice becomes widespread, a truly effective tool kit might itself become the product, forcing companies to adapt quickly to the dramatic change. Or users might abandon their status as customers altogether, collaborating to design and build their own tool kits as well as their own specialized programs.

The growing popularity of open-source software could touch off such a revolution. Consider what has happened to companies that sell software for Linux, an operating system that is virtually free. Recently, IBM took the bold step of placing $40 million of in-house tools for developing software into the public domain to encourage people to write programs that run on Linux. IBM is hoping that the move will help make Linux a widespread standard and that the company will make money by selling specialized Linux software applications, the hardware to run them, and consulting services. Other Linux companies like Red Hat are focusing on packaging, distribution, and support.

Outsourcing a portion of the innovation task to customers can be an effective approach for speeding up the development of products better suited to customer needs. The approach also holds the power to turn markets topsy-turvy, creating and shifting value at three separate levels: the industry as a whole, companies that implement the technology, and customers that take advantage of it. Exactly where that value will be generated and how it might best be captured are the multimillion-dollar questions facing companies competing in industries that are being transformed by customers as innovators.

NOTES

1. Stefan Thomke, "Enlightened Experimentation: The New Imperative for Innovation," *HBR*, February 2001

2. Eric von Hippel, "Perspective: User Toolkits for Innovation," *Journal of Product Innovation Management*, July 2001.

Innovation Blowback: Disruptive Management Practices from Asia

JOHN SEELY BROWN AND JOHN HAGEL III

In the days of the rudimentary pistol, unlucky shooters were now and then hurt when unburned gunpowder escaped back toward their faces. They came to describe this unpleasant experience as "blowback," a term that has subsequently gained wider application in military affairs—to any event that turns on its maker.

Blowback is an apt term for the unexpected consequences of the investments that Western companies have made in emerging markets. Since first entering them several decades ago, and to a remarkable extent today, these companies have tended to view them in what Kenneth Lieberthal and C. K. Prahalad[1] call "imperialistic" terms: as a beguiling mix of increasingly prosperous consumers and limitless pools of low-cost labor. Here, the thinking goes, companies can expect to harvest the fruits of the R&D and innovation skills painstakingly developed in their home countries.

That view is dangerously complacent. The very presence of Western intruders and the competition they create have inspired the emerging world's companies to raise their game in response. Far from being easy targets for exploitation, emerging markets are generating a wave of disruptive product and process innovations that are helping established companies and a new generation of entrepreneurs to achieve new price-performance levels for a range of globally traded goods and services. Eventually, such companies may capture significant market share in Europe and the United States.

To be sure, these trends are in their early development, and most companies in emerging markets face formidable obstacles to competing effectively at home, let alone penetrating the developed world. Furthermore, most Western companies haven't yet begun to serve the emerging world's low-income segments, where crucial learning takes place. Even so, early indications suggest the "innovation blowback" from emerging markets could come soon:

- Wal-Mart Stores' imports from China already account for 1 percent of its GDP. Along with other value-conscious retailers, the company stands ready to help a new breed of manufacturer target its wares at shoppers in the United States and Europe.
- Citigroup's Chinese M&A unit reports that outbound deals make up the lion's share of its pipeline—a sign that companies in China are moving abroad.
- Still more significant, mounting evidence suggests that far-sighted vanguard Western companies are not only acquiring key capabilities by serving low-income customers in

emerging markets but also preparing to use that experience to attack the growing value segments of developed markets. These companies, wielding advantages based not on factor cost differences but on superior management, show that blowback is as much an opportunity as a threat.

Most of the developed world's companies must urgently reposition themselves to deal with this offshore challenge. The solution isn't just to bring their products and business practices to the developing world, where they will invariably fail to penetrate beyond small segments of relatively affluent consumers and miss out on the vast purchasing power of less affluent ones.[2] Nor can Western companies simply strip costs from existing products. They must instead redesign their products and processes from a "clean-sheet" perspective—one that amplifies their own distinctive capabilities and those of other companies—by participating in and orchestrating networks of highly specialized businesses. In fact, they can acquire the capabilities they will soon need at home only if they face the intense competitive pressures of serving the mass market in emerging economies.

EMERGING-MARKET HOTBEDS

Emerging markets are well known for their role in activities such as assembling consumer electronics products and providing low-level customer support through burgeoning call centers. They will become even more significant as catalysts for product and process innovation.

Two powerful factors are converging to transform them into catalysts of this kind. One is the low incomes of consumers in China and India—a total of 457 million households in 2002, with an average annual income of less than $6,000 a year. The other is the spending behavior of this immense group of consumers, who, by Western standards, are unusually youthful, demanding, open-minded, and adventurous. One study cited by Lieberthal and Prahalad, for instance, showed that Indian consumers sample an average of 6.2 brands a year of a given consumer product for every 2.0 brands their US counterparts buy.[3]

These demographics and consumer traits set a stern precedent. To penetrate this vast market, companies must charge prices that the majority of its consumers can afford. Furthermore, the climate of openness implies diminished loyalty to established brands and greater receptiveness to new participants and product features. Both will force companies to rethink the way they develop and deliver their offerings.

Mobile technology demonstrates both the opportunity and the challenge. China and India, thanks to their army of early adopters, have become two of the world's largest markets for mobile phones. But these markets differ from Western ones in important ways. According to Mouli Raman, the chief technology officer of OnMobile, an entrepreneurial company spun out of Infosys Technologies three years ago, the cost of equipment for mobile-telephone networks must fall by a factor of five for it to succeed in the Indian market. Pricing for mobile-network operators must also be restructured, with smaller up-front license fees and more emphasis on performance-based payments.

Established technology vendors such as Nokia or Sony Ericsson must decide whether products designed for more developed countries will succeed if merely adapted for Asia's emerging markets or a radical new approach to product and process design is required. A growing number of such companies now acknowledge that going back to the drawing board is the only choice in Asia. Products like mobile phones comprise many interdependent systems and subsystems. When the products are designed, their features require trade-offs and agreements about diverse systems and components. Companies that attempt, say, to incorporate fewer features find that the second-order effects ripple across these previous trade-offs and agreements.

THE NEW MODELS TO FOLLOW

As Western companies strip costs from their products, they will have to rethink the processes they use to design and deliver their offerings. Many will discover that their home-market organizations are no longer the primary locus of innovation. Big global companies, after specifying the performance parameters they expect, may outsource the innovation process entirely. Contrary to the belief that multinationals must enter the emerging world in a vertically integrated fashion to ensure quality, they may begin to *disintegrate* vertically there—not just to assembly but all the way to product design. To some Western executives this might seem like a radical notion, but the practice of outsourcing innovation is gaining ground. Gateway and Hewlett-Packard, for example, recognizing that they couldn't move quickly into consumer electronics markets, have turned to original-design manufacturers in Asia for their new consumer product offerings.[4]

Companies have many ways to manage product and process innovation in emerging markets, but three are especially promising. Although presented separately, they are not mutually exclusive; a company can amplify the impact of its own capabilities, and deliver greater value at much lower cost, by combining them. The first approach is described through a cautionary tale about how Japanese motorcycle makers went to China only to get beaten at their own game. But like the cases illustrating the other approaches, this one also describes an opportunity for Western companies: to turn blowback to their advantage by building distinctive capabilities in the low-income segments of emerging economies before other companies do.

Production-Driven Modularity

Few Westerners could find Chongqing on a map. Yet this central Chinese city is home to a network of companies whose vibrant new way of designing and manufacturing motorcycles is a prototype for disruptive innovation. The network uses a distinctive management process that economists at Tokyo University, who have studied such networks in great depth, call "localized modularization"—a loosely controlled, supplier-driven approach that speeds up a company's time to market, cuts its costs, and enhances the quality of its products. The heart of this new system is a series of "process networks" mobilizing specialized companies across many levels of an extended business process. Entrepreneurial and privately owned motorcycle assemblers such as Dachangjiang, Longxin, and Cixi Zongshen Motorcycle orchestrate the networks.

These companies got their start by competing against estab-lished state-owned assemblers that had partnered with leading Japanese motorcycle makers such as Honda Motor, Suzuki Motor, and Yamaha. The private assemblers refined the Japanese com-panies' tightly integrated product architecture into one that was more flexible and modular but just as functional. The Chinese sys-tem makes it possible for the assemblers to modularize production in parallel by outsourcing components and subassemblies to inde-pendent suppliers. In contrast to more traditional, top-down ap-proaches, the assemblers succeed not by preparing detailed design drawings of components and subsystems for their suppliers but by defining only a product's key modules in rough design blueprints and specifying broad performance parameters, such as weight and size. The suppliers take collective responsibility for the detailed design of components and subsystems. Since they are free to im-provise within broad limits, they have rapidly cut their costs and improved the quality of their products.

Locating major suppliers and assemblers in the same city helps to mobilize the appropriate specializations. Informal social networks, developed in crowded teahouses and restaurants, sup-plement more formal efforts to coordinate suppliers and assem-blers. Throughout India and China, such emerging local business ecosystems play a major role in speeding up product and process innovation. In this production-driven form of modularization, suppliers of components and subassemblies—the frame, the en-gine, the suspension—take much of the responsibility for coor-dinating their work. Solving problems by combining people from diverse fields makes the solution more creative.

Thanks to these innovations, China has made rapid gains in motorcycle export markets, especially in Africa and Southeast

Asia, and now accounts for 50 percent of all global production of motorcycles. The average export price of Chinese models has dropped from $700 in the late 1990s (already several hundred dollars less than the cost of equivalent Japanese models) to under $200 in 2002. The impact on rivals has been brutal: Honda's share of Vietnam's motorcycle market, for instance, dropped from nearly 90 percent in 1997 to 30 percent in 2002. Japanese companies complain about the "stealing" of their designs, but the Chinese have redefined product architectures, in ways that go well beyond copying, by encouraging significant local innovation at the component and subsystem level.

It isn't all upside for the Chinese. Price competition has eroded the profit margins of both assemblers and suppliers, jeopardizing their ability to invest in further product innovation. Some consolidation by assemblers—plus a move into marketing and service—seems likely.

Customer-Driven Modularity

Over the years, consumer packaged-goods companies have reduced their products' unit size in emerging markets to unlock demand among consumers who can't afford bigger portions. Coca-Cola, for example, began selling 200-milliliter bottles of Coke in India in 2003; Britannia launched Tiger Biscuits in 20-gram packages in 1999. What if companies took this approach with more expensive purchases, such as mobile phones, or even with products for low-income businesses?

Cummins, the producer of diesel engines and power generators, recently did just that in India. By modularizing a product

for the distinct needs of different kinds of customers and channel partners, the company cut the total cost of ownership and of
sales in the channel. The result: higher demand for Cummins
products.

HOW CUMMINS DID IT

By 2000 the company had already captured 60 percent of the
high-horsepower end of the Indian market. But it was only a
marginal player in the large and rapidly growing low-horsepower
(under one-hundred-kilowatt) end, where buyers include small
retailers, regional hospitals, and farmers requiring an assured
power source in a country where outages are frequent. This big
market was potentially lucrative, but its demands are daunting:
each segment needs slightly different features. Farmers, for example, want engines protected against dirt, while noise is a bigger issue for hospitals. Cummins realized that it needed a
low-horsepower engine that could affordably meet the needs of
all these customers.

The company realized that it couldn't afford direct distribution, given the need for low prices. Instead it would have to use
third-party distributors, all of them less skilled than its direct
sales force and less able to help customize the product for the
needs of particular end users. The solution was to create a series
of smaller, lower-powered, modularized engines and to combine
them with add-ons called "gensets" (generation sets) that could
be customized for different segments. By packaging components
in ready-to-assemble gensets, Cummins broadened the product's
appeal to both customers and distributors. Customers liked the
gensets because the product came tailor-made; the hospital version, for instance, had a noise-abatement hood that was omitted

from the farm kit, which had dust and dirt guards not included in the hospital version. Gensets also appealed to distributors because they didn't have to source these add-ons themselves—something that would have been beyond their means and skills.

Modularizing the product to meet the needs of customers and channels also helped solve operational dilemmas. Customized products ordinarily mean smaller manufacturing runs, so Cummins faced an increase in the average unit cost of production for an offering that had to be cheap. By modularizing it, the company increased production runs of common subsystems and components, thus keeping overall costs low. It also pressed suppliers of peripherals, such as the noise-abatement hood, to standardize designs and cut costs.

Compared with the radical process innovations of the Chinese motorcycle assemblers, which outsource more of their core production, Cummins's strategy may seem familiar (see sidebar, "Beyond Big-Bang Innovation"). Western companies, after all, have long grappled with customization and "segment-of-one" challenges. Yet these efforts often end at the factory door. When modularization reflects only the need to cut manufacturing costs—rather than the problem of reaching small, dispersed segments of low-income customers through third-party channels—it typically fails to cut the cost of ownership for customers and the cost of sales in the channel.

BEYOND INDIA

The new genset engines have been an unqualified success in India, where Cummins has won 40 percent of the market over the past three years. Genset sales now account for 25 percent of the company's total power generation sales there. Despite the much lower unit prices of the new range, its net profitability is comparable to that of the high end. Exports began in 2002 to other parts of Asia and were later extended to Africa, Latin America, and the Middle East. Can it be long before Cummins introduces its low-horsepower generators in more developed markets?

If it does, it could leverage another advantage derived from competing in Asian mass markets: the high levels of reliability it had to design into the engines not only because its customers can't depend on the local power supply but also because the low prices they demand mean that its margins can't sustain an after-sales service unit. This higher reliability could prove competitively devastating in developed countries, where many vendors have competed away margins on their products and now depend on profitable aftermarkets. An attacker selling products that don't require after-sales service could dry up that profit pool.

Process-Driven Services

Innovation in emerging markets won't be limited to manufactured goods. The desire to reach vast low-income segments of Asia's population is also pushing service organizations to new levels of achievement. One vivid example comes from the Aravind Eye Care System, at Madurai, in the south Indian state of Tamil Nadu. The Aravind system—dedicated to eradicating "needless blindness by providing appropriate, compassionate, and high-quality eye care for all"—includes a chain of hospitals and a manufacturing center for sutures, synthetic lenses, and eye pharmaceuticals.

Aravind, which occupies a highly specialized health care

niche, developed efficient processes by treating huge numbers of extremely poor patients in a country where 12 million people are totally blind and an additional 8 million are blind in one eye. Its hospitals perform two hundred thousand operations a year—nearly 45 percent of all such operations in Tamil Nadu and 5 percent of those throughout India. High volumes are dictated by the affliction's scale and by the need to make the network's nonprofit hospitals viable and to generate funds for expansion.

Over the years, Aravind has carefully honed the flow of work through its outpatient departments and surgical wards—and both have reached impressive levels of efficiency. Cataract operations in Madurai, for example, are performed on four operating tables, side by side. Two doctors operate, each on two adjacent tables. When the first operation is over, the second patient is already in place. "Usually I do about 25 surgeries in a half-day session," a local doctor told the Indian writers of a case study.[5] "Most [doctors] do this number." The intense throughput doesn't seem to compromise quality. Indeed, major complication rates are highly satisfactory: in virtually all "event" categories—such as iris trauma or prolapse—Madurai's 2002 figures were better than those of the United Kingdom (as documented in a national survey by the Royal College of Ophthalmologists).

In this case, too, the need to serve low-income customers in challenging conditions spurred innovation. People in rural areas, for example, suffer from refractive blindness resulting from the prohibitive time, travel, and other incidental costs of getting a pair of glasses. Aravind studied data on the needs of patients, prepared lenses in advance, and set up mobile optical shops in remote villages so that patients could be examined near where they live and, if necessary, supplied with glasses on the spot.

Other Indian health care entrepreneurs, using processes developed in similar conditions, are already encouraging patients in more developed countries to get better value for money by traveling to Indian facilities for specialized services. Institutions such as the Narayana Hrudayalaya Foundation (a cardiac care facility in Bangalore) and Escorts Heart Institute and Research Centre, in New Delhi, are proving that services, though intangible, can be delivered in a surprisingly flexible way. A recent study by the Confederation of Indian Industry (CII) and McKinsey predicted that medical tourism in India could generate $2 billion a year in revenues by 2012.

THE IMPLICATIONS FOR WESTERN COMPANIES

These models of innovation spell out a clear message for many companies in the developed world: if you're not participating in the mass-market segment of emerging economies, you're not developing the capabilities you will need to compete back home. Our first recommendation to Western companies is therefore to go offshore, not just to the affluent segments, and not just for wage cost differentials, but to serve the mass market. Only there will you be forced to innovate in the ways required to succeed in the future. The recommendations that follow build on this basic idea.

Specialize

It was Adam Smith who first noted the power of division of labor
to increase productivity—the basis of the "dynamic economic
theory" laid out in *The Wealth of Nations*. As the economist Brian
Loasby[6] points out, the power of specialization follows not from
specialization itself but from the new capabilities it promotes.
Viewed in this way, it becomes dynamic rather than static; it enhances incentives and opportunities for further innovation.

Companies can't have all the skills needed to deliver products
or services; they must choose what they do themselves and collaborate with others for the rest. They should stick to one of three
types of activities: managing infrastructure, managing customer
relationships, or developing and commercializing innovative
products.[7] Specialization requires businesses to find partners that
enhance and complement their capabilities. Such cooperation
calls for the better coordination of resources across and within
enterprises as well as a fresh approach to managing processes.
Offshoring in emerging markets accelerates the building of capabilities on a global scale by helping companies to participate in
talent-rich process networks and then to orchestrate them.

Orchestrate Process Networks

Companies can best accelerate the building of capabilities in two
stages. The first involves setting up, accessing, developing, and
ultimately orchestrating true process networks of the kind used
by the motorcycle makers in Chongqing and, in the apparel industry, by the Hong Kong-based company Li & Fung, which

deploys a network of 7,500 specialized business partners to create customized supply chains for each new apparel line. Such process orchestrators decide which companies can participate in the network, define each party's role, and guarantee performance and fair rewards. This gatekeeper role distinguishes emerging process networks from more fluid aggregations of companies.[8]

The results are impressive. In the case of the motorcycle network, the undertaking is divided among independent activities, each with a clear owner accountable for performance. This "loose coupling" promotes flexibility (such as quicker responses to the customer's needs) and scalability (the ability to involve the largest possible number of participants and, hence, to access a wide range of specializations). Mobilizing process networks is a formidable challenge requiring robust "performance fabrics": technology- and business-based ways of reducing the cost of interaction among network participants. Successful orchestrators such as Cisco Systems, which has invested heavily in distributed learning platforms, focus hard on one key ingredient: creating shared meanings. The ability to build trust quickly is also a part of the recipe.

Orchestrate Innovation Networks

Moving from orchestrating processes to orchestrating innovation is the second stage of efforts to speed up the building of capabilities. Orchestrators like Li & Fung are learning to build them more quickly across enterprise networks, not just gaining access to specialized resources. To succeed, companies must generate the friction that shapes and sharpens learning when people of different backgrounds and skills collaborate on real problems.

Clear performance targets, an unconstrained environment for finding solutions, and the sharing of prototypes across organizational boundaries generally produce the most beneficial results. Processes must be developed, with the help of new generations of information technology, to ensure that innovations are disseminated across the network. As productive friction expands within it, a virtuous cycle reinforces shared meanings and trust.

Western companies go offshore for many reasons: among others, to cut wages (and thus costs), to gain access to distinctive skills that accelerate the building of capabilities, and to seek new markets.[9] Too often, however, investments in new markets focus only on the affluent segments of emerging economies. By targeting instead the specific and demanding needs of lower-income consumers, Western companies can address a far bigger emerging-market opportunity and create the ability to take innovative products and services from the emerging world and use them in new categories at home.

Beyond Big-Bang Innovation

When Western executives discuss innovation, they tend to focus more on products than on processes and mostly on breakthroughs rather than incremental product innovations. Supercomputers, blockbuster pharmaceuticals, fuel cells, nanotechnology, lasers—innovations like these capture the imagination and attention of executives in developed countries.

Yet very few companies create significant shareholder value through breakthrough product innovations; most economic wealth comes from more modest ones that accumulate over time. Process innovations may be even more important for building competitive advantage and generating wealth. Dell and Walmart Stores, for instance, have used them to generate enormous amounts of it.

In fact, most innovation involves creatively recombining existing components of technologies, products, or business systems. Schumpeter's "gales of creative destruction," for example, came not from isolated, discontinuous events but rather from ongoing efforts by entrepreneurs to find better ways of serving markets. Silicon Valley—for many, the epicenter of innovation—generates most of its economic wealth by incrementally enhancing technology.

If executives expand their view of innovation, they may be better prepared to see it in terms of institutional capacity and pace. For example, developing a more modular and loosely coupled product architecture—as Cummins and the Chongqing motorcycle assemblers did—increases the institutional capacity for innovation and thus promotes incremental improvement. Specialization, as in the example of the Aravind Eye Care System, helps an organization develop innovative processes more rapidly by providing it with lessons from a larger number of comparable experiences.

More important still, a broader view of innovation that values the role of incremental change communicates the power of bootstrapping. Companies that start out with limited capabilities—such as those in many developing economies—can rapidly build them over time through a series of modest process and product innovations. Ultimately, individual innovations may matter less than the institutional capacity to sustain a rapid series of improvements and the pace at which they are developed and disseminated through the network.

NOTES

1. Kenneth Lieberthal and C. K. Prahalad, "The End of Corporate Imperialism," *Harvard Business Review* 81:8 (August 2003), pp. 109–17.

2. Dell, which in the United States epitomizes innovative production processes, admitted as much when price competition from local companies forced it to retreat last August from its efforts to sell low-cost consumer PCs in China.

3. Lieberthal and Prahalad, "The End of Corporate Imperialism," pp. 109–17.

4. John Hagel III, "Offshoring Goes on the Offensive," *The McKinsey Quarterly*, 2004 Number 2, pp. 82–91.

5. Sankara Manikutty and Neharika Vohra, "Aravind Eye Care System: Giving Them the Most Precious Gift," Indian Institute of Management case study, Ahmedabad, India, 2003 (revised 2004).

6. Brian Loasby, *Knowledge, Institutions, and Evolution in Economics* (London: Routledge, 2002).

7. John Hagel III and Marc Singer, "Unbundling the Corporation," *The McKinsey Quarterly*, 2000 strategy anthology: On Strategy, pp. 147–56.

8. John Seely Brown, Scott Durchslag, and John Hagel III, "Loosening Up: How Process Networks Unlock the Power of Specialization," *The McKinsey Quarterly*, 2002 special edition: Risk and Resilience, pp. 58–69.

9. Vivek Agrawal, Diana Farrell, and Jaana K. Remes, "Offshoring and Beyond," *The McKinsey Quarterly*, 2003 special edition: Global Directions, pp. 24–35.

The Process of Social Innovation

GEOFF MULGAN

Every truth passes through three stages.
First, it is ridiculed. Second, it is violently opposed.
Third, it is accepted as being self-evident.
—ARTHUR SCHOPENHAUER

Much of what we now take for granted in social life began as radical innovation. Little more than a century ago, few believed that ordinary people could be trusted to drive cars at high speed, the idea of a national health service freely available was seen as absurdly utopian, the concept of "kindergarten" was still considered revolutionary, and only one country had given women the vote. Yet these and many other social innovations went on to make progress from the margins to the mainstream.

During some periods in recent history, civil society provided most of the impetus for social innovation (see sidebar "What Is Social Innovation"). The great wave of industrialization and urbanization in the nineteenth century was accompanied by an extraordinary upsurge of social enterprise and innovation: mutual self-help, microcredit, building societies, cooperatives, trade unions, reading clubs, and philanthropic business leaders creating model towns and model schools. In nineteenth- and early-twentieth-century Britain, civil society pioneered the most influential new models of child care, housing, community development, and social care. At other times governments have taken the lead in social innovation—for example, in the years after 1945 democratic governments built welfare states, schooling systems, and institutions using methods such as credit banks for farmers and networks of adult education colleges. (This was a period when many came to see civic and charitable organizations as too parochial, paternalist, and inefficient to meet social needs on any scale.)

There is every reason to believe that the pace of social innovation will, if anything, accelerate in the coming century. There is certainly more money flowing into NGOs and civil society than ever before. Economies in both developed and (to a lesser extent) developing countries are increasingly dominated by services rather than manufacturing. Over the next twenty years, the biggest growth for national economies is likely to come in health, education, and care, whose shares of GDP are already much greater than are those of cars, telecommunications, or steel. These growing social sectors are all fields in which commercial, voluntary, and public organizations deliver services, in which public policy plays a key role, and in which consumers co-create value alongside producers (no teacher can force students to learn if they don't want to). For all of these reasons, traditional business models of innovation are only of limited use—and much of the most important innovation of the next few decades is set to follow patterns of social innovation rather than innovation patterns developed in sectors such as information technology or insurance.

What Is Social Innovation?

Social innovation refers to innovations that are social both in their ends and in their means. Their purpose is to meet social needs and they tend to create greater social capacity to act and to be diffused through organizations whose primary purposes are social. Business innovation is generally motivated by profit maximization and diffused through organizations that are primarily motivated by profit maximization. There are, of course, very many borderline cases, for example, models of distance learning that were pioneered in social organizations but then adopted by businesses, or for-profit businesses innovating new approaches to helping disabled people into work. But these definitions provide a reasonable starting point.

A good example of a socially innovative activity in this sense is the spread of cognitive behavioral therapy, proposed in the 1960s by Aaron Beck, tested empirically in the 1970s, and then spread through professional and policy networks in the subsequent decades. A good example of socially innovative new organizations is the Big Issue, which publishes *Big Issue* magazine in the UK, and its international successor network of magazines sold by homeless people.

Thousands of recent examples of successful social innovations have moved from the margins to the mainstream. They include neighborhood nurseries and neighborhood watch groups, Wikipedia and the Open University, holistic health care and hospices, microcredit and consumer cooperatives, the fair trade movement, zero-carbon housing developments and community wind farms, restorative justice and community courts, and online self-help health groups.

Yet despite these trends, the process of social innovation re-

mains understudied. While processes of commercial innovation
have been the subject of considerable academic research, the parallel field of social innovation has received little attention and
rarely goes beyond anecdotes and vague generalizations.[1] This
neglect is mirrored by the lack of practical attention paid to social
innovation. As compared with the funds spent on commercial
and military innovation, the amount spent by governments, non-
governmental organizations, and foundations to develop innovative solutions to common needs is small. While national strategies
abound to support innovation in business and technology, no
comparable strategies at the national level exist to understand
and support social innovation.

Where Severe Innovation Deficits Exist

- Aging populations that require, for example, new ways of organizing
  pensions, care, mutual support, housing, urban design, mobility, and
  new methods of countering isolation.
- The growing diversity of countries and cities, which demands innovative ways of organizing schooling, language training, and housing,
  to avoid the risks of conflict and mutual resentment.
- The rising incidence of chronic diseases such as arthritis, depression,
  and diabetes. Some historically acute diseases (such as cancers and
  heart disease) are becoming chronic. It is widely acknowledged that
  the key solutions will have as much to do with social organization as
  with medical provision.
- Many of the behavioral problems that partly result from affluence are
  worsening, including obesity, bad diet, and inactivity, as well as
  addictions to alcohol, drugs, and gambling. None of these is easily
  addressed by traditional models.

- Difficult transitions to adulthood—there is a great need to help teen-agers successfully navigate their way into more stable careers, rela-tionships, and lifestyles.
- Crime and punishment in some countries (including the United King-dom) show a majority of convicted criminals reoffend within two years of leaving prison—a striking pattern of failure.
- The mismatch between growing GDP and stagnating happiness (and declining real welfare according to some measures).
- The glaring challenges that surround climate change—how to reor-ganize cities, transport systems, and housing to dramatically reduce carbon emissions, and how to adapt to climate change that may al-ready be irreversible.

The Young Foundation's precursors were among the world's most important centers for understanding social enterprise and innovation and for doing it. Under Michael Young, widely seen from the 1960s to the 1990s as one of the world's most effective social entrepreneurs, they helped create dozens of new institu-tions, including the Open University and its parallels around the world, the magazine *Which?*, the School for Social Entrepre-neurs, and the Economic and Social Research Council. The in-stitutions pioneered new social models such as phone-based health diagnoses, extended schooling, and patient-led health care.[2] This tradition of practical social innovation is now being energetically revived from the Young Foundation's base in east London, where we are working with cities, governments, com-panies, and NGOs to accelerate their capacity to innovate, and launching new organizations and models that can better meet people's needs for care, jobs, and homes.

The combination of our institutional heritage and current activities prompted us to seek a better understanding of social innovation—and particularly innovations that take the form of replicable programs or organizations. We are particularly interested in fields where there is the greatest gap between needs and current provision, which can often be gauged by how angry or dissatisfied people are (see sidebar "Where Severe Innovation Deficits Exist"). As the great Victorian historian Lord Macauley wrote: "There is constant improvement precisely because there is constant discontent."

This article provides a summary of our findings about the processes of social innovation and it outlines the frameworks we have developed for understanding how to accelerate social innovation and how to improve the chances of new ideas succeeding.

WHO DOES SOCIAL INNOVATION?

There are many lenses through which to understand social innovation. Today most discussion of social innovation tends to adopt one of two main lenses for understanding how change happens. In the first, social change is portrayed as having been driven by a very small number of heroic, energetic, and impatient individuals. History is told as the story of how they remade the world, persuading and cajoling the lazy and timid majority into change. Robert Owen (founder of cooperatively run factories), Octavia

Hill (inventor of many ideas of housing management, heritage protection, and community housing), and Michael Young are three exemplars drawn from British history who combined an ability to communicate complex ideas in compelling ways with a practical ability to make things happen. Countless other similar social innovators can be cited from around the world—and the leaders of social innovation have included politicians, bureaucrats, intellectuals, business people, as well as NGO activists. Some are widely celebrated—Muhammad Yunus (the founder of Grameen Bank and other microcredit enterprises), Kenyan Nobel Prize winner Wangari Maathai, and Saul Alinsky, the evangelist of community organizing in the United States.

There are also many less well-known but deeply impressive figures, such as Jeroo Billimoria, who founded the India-wide Childline, a twenty-four-hour help line and emergency response system for children in distress;[3] Vera Cordeiro, who founded Associação Saúde Criança Rensacer in Brazil;[4] and Taddy Blecher, who founded the Community and Individual Development Association (CIDA) City Campus, the first private higher education institution in South Africa to offer a virtually free business degree to students from disadvantaged backgrounds.[5] These individual stories are always inspiring, energizing, and impressive. They show just how much persistent, dedicated people can achieve against the odds, and they serve as reminders of the courage that always accompanies radical social change.

The second lens is very different. Seen through this lens, individuals are the carriers of ideas rather than originators. If we ask which innovations had the most impact over the past half century, the role of individuals quickly fades into the background.

The far-reaching movements of change, such as feminism or environmentalism, have involved millions of people and dozens of intellectual and organizational leaders, many of whom have had the humility to realize that they were often as much following as directing changes in public consciousness. As with individual innovators, these movements are rooted in ideas grown from discontent. But their histories look very different. Environmentalism, for example, grew from many different sources. Precursors in the nineteenth century include movements for protecting forests and landscapes. In the twentieth century, environmentalism spawned scientifically inspired movements to protect biodiversity, movements to counter the pollution of big companies or gain redress for their victims, movements of direct action such as Greenpeace (which itself drew on much older Quaker traditions), and Green parties around the world. Environmentalism has also spawned a huge range of social innovations, from urban recycling to community-owned wind farms.

Whether we are focusing on individuals or on broader movements, both of these lenses with which to view social innovation bring with them useful insights. Both call attention to the cultural basis for social innovation—the combination of exclusion, resentment, passion, and commitment that makes social change possible. Both also confirm that social innovations spread in an "S curve," with an early phase of slow growth among a small group of committed supporters, followed by a phase of rapid take-off, and then a slowing down as saturation and maturity are achieved. Both accounts also rightly emphasize the importance of ideas—visions of how things could be different and better. Every successful social innovator or movement has succeeded because it has planted the seeds of an idea into many minds. In the long run, ideas are more powerful than individuals or institutions; indeed, as John Maynard Keynes noted, "The world is ruled by little else."

But neither story adequately explains the complexities of social change. Change rarely happens without some brave people willing to take risks and take a stand. Leadership matters even in the most egalitarian and democratic movement. Equally important is that social change depends on many people being persuaded to abandon old habits. The great religious prophets spawned great religions because they were followed by great organizers, evangelists, and military conquerors who were able to focus their energies and create great organizations.[6]

Generating Ideas by Understanding Needs and Identifying Potential Solutions

The starting point for innovation is an idea of a need that isn't being met, coupled with an idea of how it could be met. Sometimes needs are glaringly obvious, such as hunger, homelessness, or disease. But sometimes needs are less obvious or not recognized— for example, racism or the need for protection from domestic violence—and it takes campaigners and movements to name and describe these.

Needs come to the fore in many ways—through angry individuals and groups, campaigns, and political movements as well as through careful observation. They may come from informal social movements (such as online self-help groups), religious movements (instrumental, for example, in the global campaign for debt relief in Africa), existing voluntary organizations (like the organizations for the deaf that led to the development of digital hearing aids). Some of the best innovators spot needs that aren't being adequately met by the market or the state. They are often good at talking and listening, digging below the surface to understand people's needs and dislocations, dissatisfactions, and blockages (Michael Young got many of his best ideas from random conversations on street corners, buses, and even in cemeteries). Empathy is the starting point, and ethnography is usually a more relevant formal tool than statistical analysis. Personal motivations also play a critical role: people may want to solve their own problems, and they may be motivated by the suffering of their friends or family.

Some of the most effective methods for cultivating social innovation start from the presumption that people are competent interpreters of their own lives and competent solvers of their own problems. An individual or an institution seeking to find answers to the management of chronic diseases or to the problem of alienation among teenagers may do best to find how people are themselves solving their problems. Another method is to find the people who are solving their problems against the odds—the ex-prisoners who do not reoffend or the eighteen-year-old without any qualifications who nevertheless finds a job. Looking for the "positive deviants" gives insights into what might be possible, and usually at much lower cost than top-down solutions.

Needs then have to be tied to new possibilities. New possibilities may be technological, for example, using cell phones to support banking or healthcare or using the Internet to create hyperlocal media. Indeed, the Internet is now generating a host of new business models that are set to have enormous impact in the social field from collaborative consumption to data mining.[7] Other possibilities may derive from new organizational forms, like the Community Interest Company recently launched in the UK, or the special purpose organizations increasingly used in global development (for example, in developing new drugs for HIV/AIDS). Or possibilities may derive from new knowledge. For example, we now understand the importance of early childhood development in shaping future life chances. Innovators generally have a wide peripheral vision, and they are good at spotting how apparently unrelated methods and ideas can be used together.

Few ideas emerge fully formed. Instead, innovators often try things out and then quickly adjust them in the light of experience. Tinkering seems to play a vital role in all kinds of innovation, involving trial and error, hunches, and experiments that only in retrospect look rational and planned.

New social ideas are also rarely inherently new in themselves. More often they combine ideas that had previously been separate. Examples of creative combinations include diagnostic health lines (which combined the telephone, nurses, and diagnostic software), magazines sold by homeless people, the linkage of gay rights to marriage, applying the idea of rights to animals, and the use of swipe cards for renting bicycles in transit stations. Many of the most important ideas straddle the boundaries between sectors and disciplines.

Some organizations use formal creativity methods to generate possibilities, like the six hats method devised by Edward de Bono and now used worldwide,[8] the various methods involving users developed by the design company Ideo, and the consultancy What

If?, all of which aim to free groups to think more laterally and to spot new patterns. Some of these methods force creativity. For example, they encourage developers and designers to engage with the toughest customers or those facing the most serious problems.

Creativity can be stimulated by other people's ideas, which are increasingly being collected and banked. Nicholas Albery, a regular collaborator with Michael Young, founded the Institute for Social Inventions in 1985, which produced regular editions of *The Encyclopedia of Social Inventions* and *The Book of Visions*. In 1995, Albery helped launch the Global Ideas Bank, a rich online source of ideas and experiences (it also produces regular editions of *The Global Ideas Book*).[9]

In some cases, ideas can be bought on the open market. The Web-based company Innocentive, for example, offers cash rewards for innovators who have workable solutions to problems they solve, based on an assumption that often in a neighboring sector a similar structure of problem may already have been solved. There are also now many innovation laboratories, some linked to universities, some linked to companies, and some focused on particular problems, including the MIT poverty action lab (JPAL).[10]

All societies come up with many possible social innovations. Some never get beyond a conversation in a kitchen or a bar. Many briefly take organizational form but then fade as enthusiasm dims or as it becomes obvious that the idea isn't so good after all. But the key to success is to ensure that there is as wide as possible a range of choices to draw on. As Nobel laureate Linus Pauling observed, "The way to get good ideas is to get lots of ideas and throw the bad ones away."

Developing, Prototyping, and Piloting Ideas

The second phase of any innovation process involves taking a promising idea and testing it in practice. Few plans survive their first encounter with reality. It is through action that they evolve and improve. Social innovations may be helped by formal market research or desk analysis, but progress is often achieved more quickly through turning the idea into a prototype or pilot and then galvanizing enthusiasm for it.

Social innovations are often implemented early. Because those involved are usually highly motivated, they are too impatient to wait for governments or big foundations. The experience of trying to make them work speeds up their evolution, and the power of example then turns out to be as persuasive as written argument or advocacy. For example, Michael Young usually moved very quickly to set up an embryonic organization, rather than waiting for detailed business plans and analyses. The Language Line organization, a case in point, began as two people with telephones and a tiny contract with the neighboring police station, and is now a global firm worth hundreds of millions of dollars.

A key virtue of quick prototyping is that innovations often require several goes before they work. The first outings are invariably flawed. The UK National Health challenge faces social innovation. Service took forty years to move from impossible dream to reality; the radio took a decade to find its form (its early pioneers wrongly assumed that members of the public would purchase airtime to send messages to their friends and families, as with the telephone); what became Wikipedia was a failure in its first outing.

In business, people talk of the "chasm" that innovations have to cross as they pass from being promising pilot ideas to becoming mainstream products or services. There are likely to be quite long phases when revenues are negative and when investors have to hold their nerve. Exactly the same challenge faces social innovation. Several methods have been designed to speed up this period, including faster prototyping, intensive hand-holding by venture capital companies, and the use of rigorous milestones against which funds are released. A period of uncertainty, however, is unavoidable.

There is now a much richer range of methods available for prototyping, piloting, and testing new ideas—either in real environments or in protected conditions halfway between the real world and the laboratory. The relatively free money of foundations and philanthropists can be decisive in helping ideas through this phase. Governments have also become more sophisticated in their use of evidence and knowledge,[11] with a proliferation of pilots, pathfinders, and experiments. Incubators, which have long been widespread in business, have started to take off in the public sector and among NGOs, although practice and understanding remains very patchy. Businesses have adopted new devices like three-dimensional printers, which have made it easier to turn ideas quickly into prototypes; parallel methods are being developed in the social fields to crystallize promising ideas so that they can be quickly tested.

Some ideas that seemed good on paper fall at this stage. Michael Young, for example, launched a do-it-yourself garage because he was convinced that most drivers would prefer to invest some of their time building the garage in exchange for lower costs of production. They didn't. But even failed ideas often point the way to related ideas that will succeed. As Samuel Beckett put it: "Try Again. Fail again. Fail better."

Assessing, Scaling Up, and Diffusing Good Ideas

The third stage of the social innovation process comes when an idea proves itself in practice and can then be grown, replicated, adapted, or franchised. Taking a good idea to scale requires skillful strategy and coherent vision, combined with the ability to marshal resources and support and identify the key points of leverage, the weak chinks in opponents' walls. Often the innovative and creative "bees" (social entrepreneurs or inventors) need to find supportive "trees" (big organizations with the machineries to make things happen on a big scale). That in turn may demand formal methods to persuade potential backers, including investment appraisals, impact assessments, and newer devices to judge success, such as "social returns on investment" or "blended value."

Communication is essential at this stage. Social innovators need to capture the imagination of a community of supporters through the combination of contagious courage and pragmatic persistence. Good names, along with brands, identities, and stories play a critical role. Some social innovations then spread through the organic growth of the organizations that conceived them. Some have grown through federations—including many NGOs like Age Concern or the Citizens Advice Bureau. Governments have often played the critical role in scaling up social innovations. They have unique capacities to do this by passing laws, allocating public expenditures, and conferring authority on public agencies. Businesses grow ideas through a well-established range of methods, some of which are becoming more commonly used in the social sector, including organic growth of an originating organization, franchising and licensing, and takeover of similar but less effective organizations.

This growth phase is potentially becoming much faster. With the help of the Internet, innovations can spread very quickly, and indeed there can be little point in doing local pilots because the economics of Web-based pilots may make it as inexpensive to launch on a national or continental scale. Marginal costs close to zero accelerate the growth phase—but also the phase of decline and disappearance.

Our recent work on scaling up has shown why it is so hard for social innovation to replicate, and it has pointed to more effective strategies for handling scale.

Two necessary conditions are a propitious environment and the organizational capacity to grow. These are rare with social innovations. It may take decades to create the environmental conditions for growth—persuading consumers and public agencies to pay for something new. The organizational challenges are no less severe. In charities and social enterprises, the founders who were just right for the organization during its early years are unlikely to have the right mix of skills and attitudes for a period of growth and consolidation. Often founders cling on too long, and trustees, funders, and stakeholders do not impose necessary changes. By comparison, in business the early phases of fast-growing enterprises often involve ruthless turnover of managers and executives. Indeed, growth in all sectors nearly always involves outgrowing founders. Wise founders therefore put in place robust succession plans, and very few successfully remain in executive roles for much more than a decade. Similar considerations apply to organizations that create other organizations. Christian Aid, Catholic Agency for Overseas Development, and Tearfund, for example, are all social innovations with global reach today that outgrew their founders and founding institutions (the British Council of Churches, the Catholic Women's League, and the Evangelical Alliance, respectively).

In business, the experiences of companies such as Microsoft, Procter & Gamble, and Amazon suggest that pioneers that create markets through radical innovation are almost never the companies that go on to scale up and dominate them. The skills and mind-sets required for creating a radically new market not only differ from, but actively conflict with, those needed to grow and consolidate. Big companies are often better placed to move new ideas from niche markets to mass markets, and many have concluded that they should subcontract the creation of new and radical products to start-up firms, thus concentrating their own efforts on consolidating markets and buying up companies or licenses that they see as promising.[12]

Learning and Evolving

In a fourth stage, innovations continue to change: learning and adaptation turns the ideas into forms that may be very different from the expectations of the pioneers. Experience may show unintended consequences or unexpected applications. In professions, in competitive markets, and in the public sector, there is an increasingly sophisticated understanding of how learning takes place. New models such as the collaboratives in health (used by the UK National Health Service to improve innovation and practice in fields such as cancer and primary care) and closed research groups (used, for example, by a number of major cities to analyze their transport strategies) have helped to embed innovation and improvement into fairly conservative professions.

These examples highlight innovation as a learning curve, rather than as the "Eureka!" moment of a lone genius. Ideas start off as possibilities that are only incompletely understood by their inventors. They evolve by becoming more explicit and more formalized, as best practice is worked out, and as organizations develop experience about how to make them work. This phase involves consolidation around a few core principles that can be easily communicated. Then, as the idea is implemented in new contexts, it evolves further. It forms new combinations, learning once again becomes more tacit, until another set of simpler syntheses emerge.

Some organizations appear particularly good at maintaining the momentum from innovation rather than being stuck in a particular form or market. For example, the Samaritans in Australia have become a provider of welfare services rather than just a telephone counseling service; the ECT Group in the UK started as a community transport organization and evolved into a major supplier of curbside recycling services, and it is now moving into providing primary health care services. Generally, bigger organizations have more "absorptive capacity" to learn and evolve—but small ones can gain some of this ability through the skills of their staff and through taking part in the right kind of networks.

This linear account of innovation provides a useful framework for thinking about change, but the stages are not always consecutive. Sometimes action precedes understanding. Sometimes doing things catalyzes new ideas. Feedback loops also exist between every stage, which make real innovations more like multiple spirals than straight lines. These patterns also manifest themselves differently in different sectors. Real-life innovation is a discovery process that often leaves ideas transformed and mutated, and it sometimes sees them jump from one sector to another. For example, innovations to reduce obesity can be found in public health programs, in self-help groups, and in large commercial organizations such as Weight Watchers.

COMMON PATTERNS OF SUCCESS AND FAILURE

Social innovation doesn't always happen easily, even though people are naturally inventive and curious. In some societies, social innovations are strangled at birth. This is particularly true for societies where power is tightly monopolized, where free communication is inhibited, or where there are no independent sources of money. Generally, social innovation is much more likely to happen when the right background conditions are present. For social movements, basic legal protections and status, plus open media are key. In business, social innovation can be driven by competition, open cultures, and accessible capital, and it will be impeded where capital is monopolized by urban elites or government. In politics and government, the conditions are likely to include competing parties, think tanks, innovation funds, contestable markets, and plentiful pilots, as well as creative leaders like Jaime Lerner in Curitiba or Antanas Mockus in Bogota. In social organizations, the acceleration of social innovation is aided by practitioner networks, allies in politics, strong civic organizations (from trade unions to hospitals), and the support of progressive foundations and philanthropists. And in all of these fields, global links make it much easier to learn lessons and share ideas at an early stage, with ideas moving in every direction (for example, the movement of restorative justice from Maori culture in New Zealand to mainstream practice around the world).

Most innovations in business and technology fail. So do most social innovations. Sometimes there are good reasons for failure. An idea may be too expensive, not wanted, insufficiently useful, not good enough relative to the alternatives, or flawed by unforeseen side effects. But many ideas fail not because of inherent flaws but because of the lack of adequate mechanisms to promote them, adapt them, and then scale them up. In business, there is a reasonable flow of good innovations in part because of the pull of competitive markets, but also because of public subsidy of technology and private investment in incubators, venture capital, and start-ups. The equivalent potential supports for social innovation—foundations and public agencies—are much weaker. Governments typically provide 30 to 40 percent of NGO finance in countries like the United States, Germany, the UK, France, and Japan, but these governments are generally poor at recognizing and replicating good innovations, particularly when these come from other sectors. It is notoriously difficult for government to close even failing programs and services, and there are few incentives for either politicians or officials to take up new ideas. Failure to adapt is rarely career threatening, and anyone who does promote innovations risks upsetting powerful vested interests. It's all too easy to conclude that the apparently promising new idea depends too heavily on particular circumstances such as a charismatic individual, or that the evidence just is not strong enough.

Social innovators generally find governments unresponsive. But there are also good reasons for public sectors to be cautious about innovation. Innovation must involve failure, and the appetite for failure is bound to be limited in very accountable organizations or where people's lives depend on reliability (for example, around traffic-light systems or delivery of welfare payments). In part for this reason, improved service delivery from public institutions and NGOs usually occurs via incremental improvements to existing models rather than via the invention of entirely new ones.

Innovation is therefore easier where the risks are contained, where there is evident failure, where users have choice (so that they can choose a radically different model of school or doctor rather than having it forced on them), and where expectations are carefully managed. More generally, innovation is likely to be easier when contracts for services reward outcomes achieved rather than outputs or activities, or when there is some competition or contestability rather than monopoly provision by the state. How public sectors "dock" with the social or nonprofit sector is also important, particularly given that public funding tends to overshadow other revenue sources for many innovations. Funding outcomes rather than activities helps; so, too, does funding directed to genuinely risk-taking ideas, experiments, and trials. Yet we are not aware of a single government that has developed a fully fledged machinery for accelerating social innovation in a major sector.

Public bodies usually move too slowly for impatient entrepreneurs and activists. But in one important respect they typically move too fast: far-reaching restructurings tend to be driven
through much too quickly, ignoring the long time it takes to establish new cultures, procedures, and skills, let alone new patterns of
trust.

WHY WE NEED TO KNOW MORE ABOUT SOCIAL INNOVATION

The expanding field of research on business innovation has obvious relevance to social innovation. Some of the distinctions are
relevant between total, expansionary, or evolutionary innovations,[13] or between incremental, radical, or systematic ones.[14] So
is the research on competing models,[15] the sociological work on
the role of intermediaries who help make markets work more efficiently, spotting connections and opportunities,[16] the analyses
of how much innovation is best understood as creative reinterpre-
tation,[17] and the work pioneered by Everett Rogers on diffusion.

Often the insights from business pose important challenges to
social innovators. We know, for example, that in some sectors the
best market structure for innovation seems to be a combination of
oligopolistic competition between a few big companies and a
much larger penumbra of smaller firms (the model that exists in
sectors such as microchips, software, cars, and retailing). Yet in
most social fields, monopolistic governments sit alongside small
units that are usually too small to innovate radically (schools, doc-

tors' surgeries, police stations), which may be one reason why far-reaching innovations are so rare.

We know that disaggregated industries tend to adapt better to volatility, and that big structures are better under stable conditions. We know that innovation is often serendipitous—seeking one solution, firms stumble on another, quite different one. The organizational choices faced by social and commercial organizations also run in parallel. Some companies organize innovation largely in-house as part of their mainstream business (like 3M); some create semiautonomous corporate venture units (like Nokia); some grow through acquisition of other innovative companies as well as their own innovation (Cisco for example); others use widespread networks (like the Original Design Manufacturing companies in China). Again, in the social field there are similar advantages and disadvantages in keeping innovation in-house (as, for example, in the UK National Health Service in the past), integrating innovative NGOs into big public systems (as has often happened in housing), or using networks (the traditional method of innovation in fields as diverse as public health and urban planning).

In other fields, social organizations have been ahead of business. The fashion for user networks in business innovation is emulating long-standing practices in NGOs (Michael Young pioneered patient-led health innovations a generation ago, including what became the Expert Patients Programme in the UK National Health Service); similarly the open-source methods have taken models from academia and civic organizations directly into the heart of business.[18]

Important differences also separate social innovation from innovation in business. There are likely to be very different motives, which may include material incentives but will almost certainly go far wider to include motives of recognition, compassion, identity, autonomy, and care. The critical resources are likely to be different: in businesses money provides the bottom line, but social innovations usually seek out a different mix of resources including political recognition and support, voluntary labor, and philanthropic commitment. Social organizations tend to have different patterns of growth: as a rule they don't grow as fast as private ones, but they also tend to be more resilient. Judging success is also bound to be very different. Scale or market share may matter little for a social innovation concerned with a very intense but contained need. In some of the most radical social innovations, participants' lives are dramatically improved by the act of collaboration, such as in the reorganization of social care as self-directed support.[19] These are all reasons to call for more rigor, sharper concepts, and clearer metrics in understanding social innovation.

Existing Research on Social Innovation and Related Fields

Fortunately our understanding of social innovation is not a completely barren territory. There have been many case studies of social innovations within different fields (including health, education, and criminal policy), and useful attempts have been made to understand social innovation in some universities, including Stanford, Duke, and Harvard. However, these endeavors have focused on individual case studies rather than investigating common patterns or aggregating learning.[20] As such, they have not yet provided widely acknowledged models or sufficient practical insights for practitioners: often rich accounts of individual social innovations do not add up to a clear picture of patterns (and generally the quality of theoretical work in this field has been low, with little progress since the pioneering work in the 1980s at Manchester and Sussex universities linking social innovation to broader patterns of technological change). Nor has much use been made of the advances made in parallel disciplines.

As well as the study of innovation in economics and science, there is a small emerging body of research into the capacity of formally constituted social organizations (nonprofits, NGOs, charities, and voluntary and community organizations) to innovate in the delivery of public services and to build up innovative capacity more widely.[21] The Young Foundation working with others in the Social Innovation Exchange has mapped the methods in use around the world, and shown the common patterns."[22] There is also some limited emerging work on the replication of successful voluntary sector initiatives[23]—which, though valuable, investigates one aspect of the process of innovation in isolation from its wider and precursory elements.

Considerable work is now under way on measuring the outputs and outcomes of public and social organizations, including the fascinating work led by Dale Jorgenson at Harvard on valuing the informal economy and family work, and the recent work led by Tony Atkinson at Oxford University on the value of public services. These go far beyond the rather crude claims that are sometimes made for the productivity and efficacy of social organizations. Yet the truth is that very little is known about productivity in the civic sector—and although in mature fields it is possible to compare similar public, private, and nonprofit organizations, there are few general patterns. The serious work on understanding social value and productivity is still at a very early stage, without much in the way of theoretical foundations or practical applications.

Why What We Don't Know Matters

The absence of sustained and systematic analysis is holding back the practice of social innovation. Specifically, a lack of knowledge makes it harder to see the main gaps in current provision of funding, advice, and support. This is likely to result in fewer potential innovations being initiated. A lack of knowledge about common patterns is almost certain to make it harder for innovators themselves to be effective and for ideas to be improved into a sustainable form.

The practice of social innovation remains roughly at the point where science was more than a century ago, when invention and innovation were left to the enthusiasm and energy of determined individuals like Thomas Edison and Alexander Graham Bell, who beavered away in their laboratories until the occasional "Eureka!" moment gave the world a new invention. As it came to be understood just how important science was to the economy (and to warfare), invention and innovation were taken out of the attics and garden sheds. Ideas were backed with large-scale public funding, R&D departments in big companies and university departments, and the systematic testing of new ideas became the norm. We live today with the results of that revolution, along with a stream of new products that come onto the market every year.

Social innovation has yet to pass through a similar revolution. But many are beginning to recognize that more systematic approaches pay dividends by speeding up the spread of effective solutions and reducing social costs. It is also becoming apparent to many that the key industries of the twenty-first century—health, education, and child care and eldercare, each of which will be a far larger share of GDP than information technology or cars—will require very different approaches, partly because they are so deeply shaped by public policy, and partly because they depend so much on coproduction by the user, patient, or learner.

We have proposed some of the new mechanisms and methods that may be needed. In fields where governments are the main purchasers, the more deliberate funding of outcomes rather than outputs, and the encouragement of genuine contestability, can help. But these are unlikely to be sufficient. We therefore advocate what we call "innovation accelerators": funds for seeding ideas supported by teams that combine understanding of policy contexts with understanding of business design, growth, and management (the Young Foundation's Launchpad team demonstrates how these can work in practice). We also have advocated more deliberately designed spaces in public services that encourage experimentation (such as the UK's public service zones that allowed national rules to be broken, and rewarded results rather than compliance) and incubators that deliberately focus on mining new technologies for social applications.

In all of these, social innovation is likely to be most successful when there is close involvement of people with the strongest understanding of needs and where there are sophisticated metrics of success that can reward rapid learning and evolving end goals.

The good news is that this field is advancing rapidly, moving beyond the phase of anecdotes and enthusiasms, and beyond the twin vices of excessive faith in government action on the one hand and excessive faith in heroic individuals on the other. Instead it is addressing in a more systematic way some of the barriers that stand in the way of change. Through our work at the Young Foundation, we have found that there is growing interest in this field around the world—from China, whose leaders recognize the need to speed up solutions to their profound social challenges, to the Scandinavian countries that have led the world in social innovation over the past two decades and are keen to preserve their position. It is still an emerging field, with much to learn as well as much to achieve.

NOTES

1. Rare exceptions include Tudor Rickards, *Stimulating Innovation: A Systems Approach* (London: F. Pinter, 1985); J. Gerhuny, *Social Innovation and the Division of Labour* (London: Oxford University Press, 1983); M. Njihoff, *The Political Economy of Innovation* (The Hague: Kingston, 1984).

2. Michael Young, inspiration for the Young Foundation, was judged by Harvard University's Daniel Bell as the world's "most successful entrepreneur of social enterprises," and in his work and his writings he anticipated today's interest in social enterprise and the broader question of how societies innovate. For example, see M. Young, *The Social Scientist as Innovator* (Cambridge, Mass: Abt Books, 1983).

3. Childline was founded in Bombay in 1996; by 2002 the organization was working in thirty cities. For a full account, see D. Bornstein, *How to Change the World: Social Entrepreneurs and the Power of New Ideas* (Oxford, UK: Oxford University Press, 2004).

4. Renascer provides care to poor children after they are discharged from a hospital. By 2002, Renascer had assisted six thousand children, and successor organizations assisted a further ten thousand people. Now the challenge is to transform Renascer into a reference and training center spawning and supporting cells across Brazil. For a full account, see D. Bornstein, *How to Change the World*.

5. CIDA believes itself to be the world's only "free," open-access, holistic, higher-educational facility operated and managed by its students. Students

perform all functions, from administrative duties to facilities management. Two key features of the university are (1) its partnerships with a great number of businesses in the design and delivery of all programs, and (2) the requirement of all students to return to their rural schools and communities during holidays to teach what they have learned. For a full account, see Bornstein, *How to Change the World*. See also http://www.cida.co.za (accessed May 24, 2006); Lucille Davie, "Jo'Burg's Best Kept Secret," April 8, 2002 (http://www.joburg.org.za/apn/2002/klipiviersberg.stm; accessed on May 24, 2006); and Andrea Vinassa writing on http://www.workinfo.com/free/Downloads/243.htm> (accessed May 24, 2006).

6. For comparisons between business and the social sector in making organizations great, see http://www.jimcollins.com/lib/articles.html#.

7. For details about the open-source business model, see *The Economist*, "Open, but Not as Usual," http://www.economist.com/business/displaystory.cfm?story_id=5624944 (accessed May 24, 2006).

8. For example, see E. de Bono, *Lateral Thinking—Creativity Step by Step* (London: Perennial Library, 1970).

9. See Global Ideas Bank, http://www.globalideasbank.org/site/home/. The top five hundred ideas that will change the world are at http://www.globalideasbank.org/site/store/detail.php?articleId=178. For a list of similar organizations, see Stuart C. Dodd Institute for Social Innovation, http://www.stuartcdoddinstitute.org/innovationlinks.shtml (accessed May 26, 2006).

10. See generally: Poverty Action Lab, http://www.povertyactionlab.org/; Social Action Laboratory, http://www.psych.unimelb.edu.au/research/labs/soc_actionlab.html; Affirmative Action Laboratory, http://www.naledi.org.za/pubs/2000/indicator/article4.htm; Innovation Lab Copenhagen, http://www.innovationlab.net/sw4918.asp; Civic Innovation Lab, http://www.civicinnovationlab.org/; Eastman Innovation Lab, http://www.eastman.com/innovationlab/; MIT Community Innovation Lab, http://web.mit.edu/cilab/; ETSU Innovation Lab, http://www.etsu.edu/innovationlab/.

11. G. Mulgan, "Government and Knowledge," *Evidence and Policy Journal* 1:2 (May 2005), pp. 215–226.

12. C. Markides and P. Geroski, *Fast Second: How Smart Companies Bypass Radical Innovation to Enter and Dominate New Markets* (San Francisco: Jossey-Bass, 2005).

13. R. M. Walker, E. Jeanes, and R. O. Rowlands, "Measuring Innovation—Applying the Literature-Based Innovation Output Indicator to Public Services," *Public Administration* 80 (2002), pp. 201–214.

14. D. Albury and G. Mulgan, *Innovation in the Public Sector* (London: Strategy Unit, Cabinet Office, 2003).

15. Two good general sources are the Stanford Project on Emerging Companies, http://www.gsb.stanford.edu/SPEC/index.html (accessed May 25, 2006), and the Wharton School's Innovation and Entrepreneurship, http://knowledge.wharton.upenn.edu/index.cfm?fa=viewCat&CID=12.

16. J. P. Murmann, *Knowledge and Competitive Advantage: The Coevolution of Firms, Technology and National Institutions* (London: Cambridge University Press, 2004); E. von Hippel, *Democratising Innovation* (Cambridge, Mass.: MIT Press, 2005); R. Baumol, *The Free-Market Innovation Machine: Analyzing the Growth of Miracle Capitalism* (Princeton, N.J.: Princeton University Press 2003).

17. R. Lester and M. Piore, *Innovation—the Missing Dimension* (Cambridge, Mass.: Harvard University Press, 2004).

18. For a thorough analysis of open-source methods and their great potential, see G. Mulgan and T. Steinberg, *Wide Open: The Potential of Open Source Methods* (London: Demos and the Young Foundation, 2005).

19. In the UK, the In Control pilots delivered under the government's policy Valuing People and now recommended for wider adoption is a good example of innovation in the new relationship between user and suppliers. Prime Minister's Strategy Unit, Improving the Life Chances of Disabled People, January 2005, p. 93; David Brindle, "Controlling Interest," *Society Guardian*, March 2, 2005; See also http://www.in-control.org.uk/ (accessed May 25, 2006).

20. See, for example, Stanford Social Innovation Review, http://www.ssireview.com (accessed May 25, 2006); the Social Innovation Forum, http://www.wfs.org/innovate.htm (accessed May 25, 2006); Government Innovators Network, http://www.innovations.harvard.edu (accessed May 25, 2006); Changemakers, http://www.changemakers.net (accessed May 25, 2006); Leader to Leader Institute, http://www.pfdf.org/innovation/ (accessed May 25, 2006).

21. For innovations in the delivery of public services, see for example: P. Alcock, T. Barnwell, and L. Ross, *Formality or Flexibility? Voluntary Sector Contracting* (London: National Council for Voluntary Organizations, 2004); S. Osborne,

Voluntary Organizations and Innovation in Public Services (London: Routledge, 1998). For general capacity building, see E. Evans and J. Saxton, *Innovation Rules! A Roadmap to Creativity and Innovation for Not-for-Profit Organizations* (London: NFP Synergy, 2004).

22. Mulgan, et al., "In and Out of Sync: Growing Social Innovaions" (NESTA and the Young Foundation, London, 2008).

    See "The Open Book of Social Innovation." (NESTA and the Young Foundation, London, 2010).

23. D. Leat, *Replicating Successful Voluntary Sector Projects* (London: Association of Charitable Foundations, 2003); Community Action Network's beanstalk program http://www.can-online.org.uk (accessed May 25, 2006).

    This paper draws on a report titled "Social Silicon Valleys: A Manifesto for Social Innovation," available for download from <http://www.youngfoundation.org>.

Venturesome Consumption

AMAR BHIDÉ

Why is the United States a good place to innovate? The question has attracted considerable attention in recent years, particularly in Europe and Japan. Much of the writing on this topic emphasizes "supply side" factors such as the availability of venture capital, the IPO (initial public offering) market, the rule of law, and the enforcement of intellectual property rights. In this article, I will offer a complementary, "demand side" perspective, focusing on the frequently neglected role that consumers play in the multiplayer innovation game.

My interest in the purchase and use of the new technologies dates to 1982, when, as an employee of the consulting firm of McKinsey & Co., I worked on a study to help the European Union promote the IT industry. The team focused almost entirely on what the EU could do to help the producers of IT equipment through grants, subsidies, and tax breaks. Among the questions extensively debated was who was friend or foe: were U.S. companies that had extensive operations in Europe sufficiently European to deserve the EU's largesse? My efforts to broaden the scope of the study to include the behavior and needs of IT users—who were *all* in Europe—were futile. I was the lowest-ranking consultant on the team, and the clients for the study had no interest. I then wrote a *Harvard Business Review* article about the nature of the demand for innovative products, but it had a similarly negligible impact.[1]

My views have subsequently been informed by my studies over the last twenty years of new and emerging ("entrepreneurial") businesses. Obviously, entrepreneurs are more willing to innovate—and devote resources to marketing and selling their innovations—if they anticipate a large market for their product. Developers of products that have to be tailored for a particular market or require costly sales efforts are naturally concerned about whether customers will be receptive. But that's not all: I have observed the subtle role of customers, which goes beyond the decision whether or not to buy. As we will see in this article, they play an important "venturesome" role, rather like the one played by the developers of the products they use.

Although users' role in the innovation games if often neglected, my overall thesis is not new. Several economic historians have examined the close relationship between technology adoption and economic development. Among them are Mokyr[2] and Rosenberg and Birdzell,[3] who argue that the West grew rich first because people there were more open to new technologies than elsewhere. I use contemporary examples to argue that adopting technology, especially of IT by the service sector, continues to play a critical role in maintaining the prosperity of the United States and other advanced countries.

My argument also incorporates the notion of what is often now called "absorptive capacity" for innovations. The term has been used in the economic-development literature at least since the early 1960s to refer to the limited capacity of "backward" countries to put new investments (and the innovations they may embody) into productive use. Cohen and Levinthal[4] applied the term to the ability of individual firms to effectively absorb new technologies, and this usage has since become commonplace. Although their definition is broad, Cohen and Levinthal and subsequent researchers focus mainly on high-tech firms, examining, for instance, how internal R&D efforts help firms use research produced in university labs. I focus on organizations (and individual consumers) that have no formal R&D efforts and who use mid- and ground-level products rather than high-level scientific knowledge.

CONTRIBUTIONS TO PRODUCT DEVELOPMENT

MIT's Eric Von Hippel has been a leading proponent of the view that innovation often starts with users, particularly the so-called lead users, rather than the manufacturers of products. In 1988 Von Hippel reported that users had developed about 80 percent of the most important innovations in scientific instruments, as well as most of the major innovations in semiconductor processing. In *Democratizing Innovation*, published in 2005, Von Hippel writes that "a growing body of empirical work shows that users are the first to develop many and perhaps most new industrial and consumer products."

The book recalls Adam Smith's observation that manual labor-saving machines were invented by "common workmen" who "naturally turned their thoughts toward finding out easier and readier methods of performing" simple operations.[5] Von Hippel cites other examples of important innovations led by users: basic machine tools such as lathes and milling machines, oil refining, and the most widely licensed chemical processes.

In consuming products, Von Hippel provides examples from sports such as snow boarding, mountain biking, and high-performance wind surfing, which got its start when competitors in traditional wind-surfing events modified standard boards to do jumps. Their modifications were then used in boards used for normal wind surfing. Similarly, Von Hippel reports that mountain biking started in the early 1970s with young cyclists who built their own bicycles out of strong frames, balloon tires, and drum brakes from motorcycles for rough, off-road use. A fragmented cottage industry began supplying such cycles for those who didn't want to assemble their own machines: it wasn't until mountain biking had grown to a sport with half a million adherents that mainstream suppliers got into the act. Von Hippel also argues that, in general, "the contribution of users is growing steadily larger as a result of continuing advances in computer and communications capabilities."

In my research of entrepreneurial businesses over the last twenty years, I have not found user-led innovation to be widespread. At the same time I have observed that users do often play an important "venturesome" role in the development of new products even if they don't lead or initiate the development.

In the current study of VC-backed businesses I saw virtually no evidence of user-led innovation except in the very broad sense that most innovators do put themselves in the shoes of users (but if we were to count that as user-led innovation, the category would mean nothing). Nor did I encounter much user-led innovation in my previous research on *Inc.* 500 companies, nor in several hundred other ad-hoc studies I have undertaken. This could be an artifact of my samples, of course. Or it could be that claims about the ubiquity of user-led innovation may be pushed by a "man-bites-dog" bias in the academic literature—studies of *producer*-led innovation would not excite much interest.

The current study of venture-backed businesses did, however, reveal other important roles that users play in the innovation game. Developers, especially developers of mid-level products, engaged closely with so-called alpha or beta users. The engagement was far more intense than is common in focus groups and market research questionnaires (which involve hypothetical questions) or even in taste tests (with actual products). Users participated in ongoing dialogue with development teams that helped determine the attributes of the product or services that was ultimately sold.

Developers might start with the core component of a solution to an important problem faced by potential customers, but in their dialogue with users learn about complementary functions that must be added to the core to make it work. Or developers might conceive of a product with many functions, but learn that some features add more cost than value. Similarly, customer dialogue can contribute to designing an effective user interface; as the success of Google's search engine and Apple's iPod shows, the look and feel of a product can be as important to its utility as the technical features that lie "under the hood." According to many of our interviewees, many things learned from interactions with customers were incorporated into their products rather than their core idea (or patent), and this was the most valuable source of their intellectual property.

The contribution of customers to the development process tends to continue after the first commercial launch. As Rosenberg (and others) have pointed out, products can evolve so much over time that their relationship to antecedents may be unrecognizable. The first automobiles were so rudimentary that they could only be used by a "few buffs riding around the countryside terrifying horses."[6] Today's personal computers have come a long way from the pioneering Altair; its aficionados derived less practical use from their machines than did turn-of-the-century automobile buffs. Lacking basic input or output devices (such as keyboards and printers), Altairs could not even scare horses. According to Rosenberg, "learning by using" by customers often plays a significant role in transforming products from rudimentary to refined.[7]

Users may also find new applications for existing technologies. A typical automobile, for instance, now contains scores of embedded microprocessors. Similarly, consumer electronics companies have also embedded microprocessors in household appliances, sound systems, and telephones. Producers of laptops, PDAs, and electric vehicles have found new uses for innovative battery technologies. As users try to adapt new technologies for their specific applications, the technologies may gain new features (in addition to a larger market) that make them more versatile and less expensive. In other words, the initiative of users can make technologies developed for a few markets into more general purpose platforms.*

BEARING "UNMEASURABLE AND UNQUANTIFIABLE" RISKS

According to Knight's theory, the essence of entrepreneurship involves responsibility for uncertainty—facing unmeasurable and unquantifiable risk rather than betting on situations where the odds have been well established by prior trials. But it is not just the producers of an innovation who face Knightian uncertainty—purchasers also cannot form objective estimates of their risks and returns.

One source of uncertainty lies in whether an innovation actually does what it is supposed to do. A product that works in the lab or in a few beta sites may not work for all users because of differences in the condition of its implementation; a product that works fine at the outset may fail later. An innovation, like a theory, can never be proven to be "good"—at any moment, we can only observe the absence of evidence of unsoundness. Repeated use of a product may bring to the surface hidden defects that

---

* I don't want to exaggerate this effect, however—many, possibly most, of the new critical applications for crucial general-purpose technologies such as steam engines and electric dynamos were not initiated by users (except in some all-inclusive sense of the term).

cause malfunctions, increase operating costs, or pose health and safety hazards to the user or the environment.

Unanticipated technical failures injure not only developers but users of innovations. In many products and services, failures can cost users many times the purchase price. Defects in a word-processing or email package that costs just a few hundred dollars may wipe out many years of invaluable files and correspondence. Even if data isn't lost, the costs of transferring files to a new software package—and learning how to use it—can be substantial. Similarly, a defective battery in a laptop can start a fire that burns down a house (this did, in fact, happen to a friend). Tires that wear badly can have fatal consequences. A security hole in its servers can cripple an online brokerage, and the belated discovery of the hazards of asbestos can lead to tens of billions of dollars in removal costs.

Consumers face risk if they invest in new products that work perfectly well for them but fail to attract a critical mass of other users. If that happens, vendors (and providers of complementary add-ons) often abandon the product and stop providing critical maintenance, upgrades, and spare parts. Or vendors may go out of business entirely—a common occurrence in IT. Customers may be left stranded if upgrades and new releases don't have "backward compatibility" with their forebears, or if a new technology makes an old product obsolete.

Customers also face Knightian uncertainty about the value of an innovation in relation to its price. In the schema of neoclassical economics, consumers have a gigantic, well-specified utility function for all gods, extant as well as not yet invented. Therefore, when an innovation that serves a new want (or a new combination of old wants) appears, consumers consult their utility functions, as they might a tax table, and know exactly its worth to them. To my knowledge, there is not empirical basis for such an assumption. In fact, evidence from "behavioral" researchers such as George Lowenstein points in exactly the opposite direction: people don't have a clue about the value of things they have never experienced. When researchers ask subjects how much they would pay for some novel experience, such as kissing their favorite movie star, they receive whimsical responses, anchored to some irrelevant piece of data just planted in the subject's mind by the researcher, such as Social Security numbers. One interpretation of these behavioral experiments is that people are irrational; another is that they simply don't know and blurt out the first thing that comes to mind to earn their five dollars for participating in the experiment. ("Snappy answer to stupid questions," a long-ago feature from *Mad* magazine, comes to mind.)

Behavioral research has been criticized for experiments in which subjects, unlike actors in the real world, have no stake in the outcome, but in this instance the experiments do seem to correspond to reality. It is improbable, for instance, that anyone who wears glasses or contact lenses has a firm grasp of the economic value of (successful) corrective laser surgery, or that someone who has a conventional TV can gauge the value of switching to a higher-definition digital product. Indeed, I am skeptical that people who actually have laser surgery or buy a digital TV can quantify the value. Before or after a purchase, the enhanced utility is a shot in the dark, much like the value of the pleasure Lowenstein's subjects anticipate from kissing movie stars. I personally have not seriously considered either laser surgery or buying a high-definition TV, but I have been enticed by the latest in the personal computer hardware and software for more than two decades. I have no idea of the value of my numerous upgrades (or for that matter, a good estimate of the time and opportunity costs I have incurred).

Similarly, although I have worried about—and periodically endured—the consequences of technical defects and abandonment of favorite programs by vendors, I have never actually made an effort to quantify the probability distributions. I cannot imagine being able to enumerate all the dire possibilities. People who have corrective eye surgery may ask about the probability that something might go wrong or that the operation won't give them 20/20 vision. But what basics could they possibly have for evaluating the consequences twenty or thirty years later?

Organizations that purchase expensive systems do often expend many person-years' effort to evaluate their costs and benefits. For example, Columbia Business School recently acquired a new "courseware" platform. A committee was formed, long Requests for Proposals issued, shortlists made, vendor proposals studied, consultants retained . . . but for all the effort and availability of the finest analytical minds, the value of the new courseware was— and will remain—elusive. The monetary value of enhancing student satisfaction and learning and of saving faculty time can only be a blind guess. Similarly, although the out-of-pocket costs of purchasing a system played a role in picking a vendor, the magnitude of the much larger "all in" opportunity costs (e.g., the time of faculty and staff) of switching to any new courseware platform were unfathomable.

Assessing the costs and benefits of enterprise-wide software and systems used by corporations that are many times the size of the Columbia Business School is even more difficult. As the sidebar "Evaluating ERP Systems" indicates, the off-the-shelf enter-

prise software rarely matches the practices and processes that it is supposed to facilitate or automate. Rather, organizations have to extensively modify and adapt both the software and their practices. The costs of modifying the software, and the frequently more problematic "reengineering" of the practices, are very hard to pin down. So are the benefits: these are supposed to include not just the improvements realized through automation, but also the adoption of superior practices.

Evaluating ERP Systems

According to the current Wikipedia entry on the topic, ERP (enterprise resource planning) software is used for the "control of many business activities, like sales, delivery, billing, production, inventory management, quality management, and human resource management." The systems are supposed to integrate many functions, including "manufacturing, warehousing, logistics, Information Technology, accounting, human resources, marketing and strategic management." In principle, all these activities and functions use a single database rather than, for instance, the human resources department and the payroll department maintaining records on the same employee in two different and incompatible databases.

Most ERP systems are not built to suit—rather they are based on packages provided by software companies such as Oracle and SAP. The premise of such systems, according to Eric Roberts, professor of computer science at Stanford, is that "software systems are expensive and complex. What's more, the expense of a software system lies almost entirely in its development; once a system is built and tested, the marginal cost of delivering that same system to other users is typically quite small. The concentration of cost in the development phase creates a strong incentive to share development expenses over a large user base. If it costs $10 million to develop a system, it seems foolish for a single institution to bear that cost alone. Given that the bulk of that $10 million represents development, it makes far more sense—at least in theory—for a consortium of institutions to purchase software from a vendor that can then distribute those costs over the community of users."[8]

There is, however, a catch, writes Roberts: "The success of any enterprise system depends on refashioning the business practices of the institution to match the software rather than trying to change the software to accommodate the idiosyncrasies of the institution. Changing the software violates the underlying economic assumption that allows for the reduction in cost. If each institution tailors the system to suit its needs, the cost advantage vanishes."

Enterprise software vendors claim that their systems incorporate the best possible business practices. Therefore, customers gain significant advantages if they refashion their business practices to fit the standard package. But in fact, although the packages draw their "best practices" from a variety of industries and situations, there can be a considerable gap between the best-practice configuration available in the package and the practice that works best for a particular organization. In *The ABCs of ERP*, Christopher Koch comments, "While most packages are exhaustively comprehensive, each industry has quirks that make it unique. Most ERP systems were designed to be used by discrete manufacturing companies (that make physical things that can be counted), which immediately left all the process manufacturers (oil, chemical and utility companies that measure their products by flow rather than individual units) out in the cold."

In fact, it is simply infeasible for organizations to adopt all of the specified best practices. Therefore, they usually compromise: organiza-

continued...

tions change some of their best practices to suit the system, but they also "struggle" to "modify" core ERP programs to their needs, writes Koch. All this makes it extremely difficult to assess the value or the costs. Koch writes that "the value of the systems is hard to pin down because . . . the software is less important than the changes companies make in the ways they do business. If you use ERP to improve the ways your people take orders and manufacture, ship and bill for goods, you will see value from the software. If you simply install the software without trying to improve the ways people do their jobs, you may not see any value at all—indeed, the new software could slow you down by simply replacing the old software that everyone knew with the new software that no one does."

Similarly, there "aren't any good numbers to predict the costs because the software installation has so many variables, such as: the number of divisions it will serve, the number of modules installed, the amount of integration that will be required with existing systems, the readiness of the company to change, and the ambition of the project— if the project is truly meant to be a battering ram for reengineering how the company does its most important work, the project will cost much more and take much longer than one in which ERP is simply replacing an old transaction system. There is a sketchy rule of thumb that experts have used for years to predict ERP installation costs, which is that the installation will cost about six times as much as the software license. But this has become increasingly less relevant. . . . Research companies don't even bother trying to predict costs anymore.

GROUND-LEVEL DEVELOPMENT

The effective use of innovation usually requires acquiring or developing ground-level know-how. There are very few products that humans can use immediately: we have to acquire the knowledge, and sometimes the taste, for almost everything that we consume in our daily lives—we must learn how to brush our teeth, tie our shoelaces, knot ties, savor espressos, and drive cars. An innovative biometric lock opened by swiping one's fingers over a sensor eliminates losing or fumbling with keys, but there is a catch. As Anne Eisenberg (who reviewed the product for the *New York Times*) discovered, after installing the lock, she could not recall the finger-swiping technique the next day. "I swiped and swiped," she writes, "but the door wouldn't budge. Many speeds and angles can be used in swiping a finger I gradually realized, and I could no longer recapture the technique I'd used the night before." Swiping a finger isn't necessarily harder than turning a physical key in a conventional lock; but as Stephanie Schuckers, a professor of electrical and computer engineering points out, people have already learned to use standard locks: "We are all trained how to use keys, from when we are young."[9]

Differences in how products are used require consumers to do more than just acquire the knowledge of a "standard technique"—they have to develop ground-level know-how tailored to their specific requirements. For instance, users of spreadsheets don't just acquire the knowledge of standard pull-down menus and commands; they also have to develop, or at least modify, their own templates and models. Furthermore, mid-level products that are jointly used by several individuals often require the development of ground-level organizational know-how as well as technical know-how—as previously mentioned, the use of enterprise software requires the development of new processes and practices as well as adaptation of the software itself. And because processes and practices can vary considerably, each organization has to develop its own.

Research[10] on the adoption of client/server technology documents the importance of developing multifaceted ground-level know-how (which Bresnahan and Greenstein call "co-invention").* Bresnahan and Greenstein found that companies in the vanguard of adoption were in science and engineering-based industries that were "least tied to complex business procedures." The slowest adopters were in industries with great "organizational complexity," where "organizational adjustment costs were highest. Adjustment costs, rather than the benefits of client/server systems, seemed to drive the adoption of the technology.

Innovators who develop mid-level "combinations" require different skills and human capital than do researchers who work on high-level scientific problems. Similarly, users who have to de-

---

* Bresnahan and Greenstein distinguish between "invention" by producers and "co-invention" by users. Their distinction corresponds to higher and lower levels of know-how in my framework. In principle, I ought to defer to Bresnahan and Greenstein's prior terminology, especially since virtually everything in their paper is congruent with my thesis. Their language makes me uncomfortable, however, as I have said (and as Bresnahan and Greeinstein note), innovations such as client/ server technology are also "co-invented" by producers and users.

velop ground-level know-how require yet another set of skills—while technical knowledge is certainly necessary, managerial and organizational knowledge is crucial, and there are policy implications of these differences. But here I want to emphasize the following similarity: both the developers and users of innovations often require a high degree of venturesome or entrepreneurial resourcefulness in problem solving.

Developers of innovation often face situations that require such resourcefulness in the following sense: although the situation may be similar to ones the innovator has faced before, it also contains novel elements, so the innovator cannot simply repeat what has worked in the past. Experience (or "human capital"), which we may think of as the accumulated knowledge of similar past situations, helps, but it is not enough. An innovator is more than just a skilled and knowledgeable surgeon performing difficult but routine arthroscopic knee surgery. The innovator must also act resourcefully in the face of novel situations with a can-do attitude, imagination, willingness to experiment, and so on.

Consuming something novel does not always require resourceful problem solving. Drinking a new soft drink or showing up for an appointment for corrective surgery is not especially demanding. Other kinds of consumption—such as assembling a model airplane—may require patience, dexterity, and experience, but as long as the instructions are clear and complete, they do not require resourcefulness or creativity. Indeed, creative deviations from prescribed instructions can lead to undesirable outcomes. But not all innovations come with clear and complete instructions. High-tech products, especially those with complex architectures and features, rarely do, and deriving utility from them requires a great deal of resourceful problem solving.

Manuals for Windows-based personal computers and software, for instance, are famously bewildering. This is not mainly because of the incompetence of the authors of the manuals. In considerable measure, the sometimes bewildering instructions reflect the complexity of the internal architecture of the systems, the many options and features they contain, and the difficulty of anticipating how the components will interact. But whatever the cause of that impenetrability, my experience has been that the alluring features of new products rarely work "out of the box" if one simply follows the instruction manual. I have spent countless hours getting new gizmos to work, or trying to stop inexplicable crashes. And the toil is far from mechanical: I have to guess what might be wrong, conduct experiments, and troll through postings of user groups on the Internet trying to find solutions to similar problems. Moreover, figuring out how something is supposed to work is often only half the battle: in many innovations, users have to figure out how to make the product work well for *them*. In the case of innovations such as enterprise software, the figuring out involves the solving of technical and organizational problems. Experience and effort is helpful, even necessary. But as "Using ERP Systems" indicates, because the problems tend to be idiosyncratic, the solutions require a great deal of resourcefulness as well.

Using ERP Systems

The effective use of complex enterprise software requires solving both technical and organizational problems. As Koch writes:

> The inherent difficulties of implementing something as complex as ERP is like, well, teaching an elephant to do the hoochy-kootchy. The packages are built from database tables, thousand of them, that IS programmers and end users must set to match their business processes; each table has a decision "switch" that leads the software down one decision path or another . . . [F]iguring out precisely how to set all the switches in the tables requires a deep understanding of the . . . processes being used to operate the business.

Inevitably, business processes themselves have to be "reengineered." Users who want to take advantage of off-the-shelf software packages must align their processes with the "best practices" built into the software. To have a system that is truly enterprise-wide, organizations have to figure out processes that work best across their different units. Inevitably, individuals and organizational subunits resist changing the way they do things; and even if they don't, business processes and their associated information systems cannot be changed overnight. Therefore, in addition to figuring out what their business processes should ultimately look like (and how the "switches" in the software need to be set to match the processes), organizations also need to resolve how they will overcome resistance to change and make the transition from "legacy" processes and systems.

Consultants who have implemented ERP systems in the past can help ameliorate these problems. However, the issues facing different organizations are never identical, so the consultants and their clients have to solve many novel problems. Moreover, ERP packages and the other applications—for instance supply-chain, customer-relationship-

continued . . .

management (CRM), and e-commerce software—that ERP is supposed to complement also change frequently, which adds to the difficulty of deriving a tried-and-tested formula for implementation. Researchers and industry experts who have expended considerable effort to investigate what works and what doesn't have been unable to get beyond long and wooly lists. Somers and Nelson formulated a list of twenty-four "critical success factors," starting with "top management support" and including items such as "project team competence," "interdepartmental cooperation," and "clear goals and objectives."[11] For obvious reasons, such lists do little to obviate the need for situation-specific problem solving.

The mixed record of ERP systems also points to the difficult problems users must solve to realize the potential benefits. Holland and Light point out that successful implementations at pioneer New Media Technologies and Monsanto have been well publicized, but "less successful projects have led to bankruptcy proceedings and litigation."[12] Similarly, Plan and Wilcocks note the success of ERP at companies such as Cisco as well as "spectacular" failures at Hersey Foods and FoxMeyer and disappointments at Volkswagen, Whirlpool and W.L. Gore.[13]

NOT QUITE FREE

Economists often believe that innovations are a gift to consumers. Stanford's Paul Romer writes that innovators "have brought the cost of a transistor down to less than a millionth of its former level. Yet, most of the benefits from those discoveries have been reaped not by the innovating firms, but by the users of the transistors. In 1985, I paid a thousand dollars per million transistors for memory in my computer. In 2005, I paid less than ten dollars per million, and yet I did nothing to deserve or help pay for this windfall."

My analysis suggests a slightly different view. In all likelihood, users do secure the lion's share of the benefit for successful innovations. But not all innovations are successful. Apple's iPod has been a resounding success for both the company and its customers— its Lisa and Newton were not. When products fail, the downside faced by users in the aggregate (and sometimes even individually) in innovations ranging from corrective laser surgery to enterprise software matches or exceeds the downside of the innovator. Indeed, one important challenge faced by innovators is to persuade entrepreneurs to take a chance on innovations in the absence of any hard demonstration that the returns are worth the risks.

One of the notable features of the modern innovation system lies in the great many individuals and organizations that are willing to be so persuaded. At the dawn of the automobile era, only a few very rich buffs served as guinea pigs. Now, the not-so-well-off borrow against their credit cards—or spend what they "save" by buying paper napkins in bulk at Walmart—to take their chances on laser surgery and flat panel TVs without much foreknowledge of the utility of their purchase. Similarly, large corporations run by the book with the help of squadrons of financial analysts will spend tens of millions of dollars on enterprise software based on the crudest of guesses of costs and benefits.

Even late adopters who only buy tried-and-tested products don't get a free ride. Romer sells himself—and other computer users—short in declaring that they have "done nothing" to deserve the windfall of lower prices. Large markets and the prospect of their continued growth have helped drive down prices. And markets have grown because individuals and companies have invested in learning how to use computers and developed ground-level know-how. The investment is not trivial. The prices of computers have declined, but their complexity hasn't. Feature bloat may, in fact, have made computers and programs harder to use. Yet the number of people who have made the effort—possibly incurring opportunity costs many times the purchase price of their equipment and software—has over the years continued to grow. Users who build their own templates and models for spreadsheet and database programs now number in the tens of millions, whereas the teams at Microsoft who develop such products number in the thousands.

A Multitude of User Programmers

Scaffidi, Shaw, and Myers (from Carnegie Mellon's school of computer science) use a variety of sources to estimate the number of end users of computers and end-user programmers in the United States. They get a lower bound estimate of 55 million computer users in 2005 by multiplying the number of individuals in different occupational categories in 2005 by the percentage of computer users in that category in 1989. For instance, in 2005, there were about 36.7 million workers in the "managerial and professional" category, and 56.2 percent of such workers used computers in 1989, leading to an estimate of 20.6 million "managers and professionals" using computers in 2005. But as Scaffidi and coauthors point out, the percentage of computer usage in the different categories has increased significantly since 1989. For instance, the percentage of managers and professionals using computers grew from 56.2 percent in 1989 to over 70 percent in 1997. Extrapolating from these trends, the researchers arrive at an estimate of 81 million users of computers at work in 2005. They note that other estimates are even higher—for instance, a Forrester Research survey commissioned by Microsoft estimated that 129 million people in the United States between the ages of eighteen and sixty-four used computers at home or at work in 2003.

Scaffidi and coauthors also highlight the growth of some kind of programming by end users. Since 1989, the Current Population Survey (CPS) conducted by the Bureau of Census has included questions such as "Do you do programming?" and "Do you use spreadsheets or databases?" Here, too, we find substantial increases: The percentage of U.S. workers who said they used spreadsheets grew from about 10 percent in 1989 to over 30 percent in 1997. Similar increases were reported in the usage of databases. Between 1997 and 2001, "Usage of end user programming environments continued to explode, with over 60 percent of American end user workers reporting that they 'used spreadsheets or databases' in 2001. This amounted to over 45 million end users of spreadsheets or databases." Increases in the proportion of workers who reported they "did programming" were relatively modest, rising from about 10 percent of the workforce in 1989 to 15 percent in 2001. Nonetheless, the estimated 11 million workers who reported that they did programming was more than five times less than the two million programmers in the United States in 2001.[14] Of these software professionals, two-thirds worked for IT-using companies rather than IT-producing companies.[15]

CONCLUDING COMMENTS

In the North-South trade models—as in most mainstream economic theories—users of new technologies are at once passive and omniscient. They play no role in the development of innovations, but once innovations appear, users know whether they should buy the offering and what they should pay. Even in Schumpeter's theories (which in other ways challenge mainstream models), the innovator is the star, while those who imitate or modify have secondary parts. Consumers don't appear in the cast.

The neoclassical and Schumpeterian models both fail to do justice to the role of users. In a system where innovations are carried out by numerous players, the producers of innovations are, except for the end consumers, also users of higher-level or "adjacent" innovations. Users—including those at the end of the line—often play a venturesome or "entrepreneurial" role in the design of new products, bearing "unmeasurable and unquantifiable" risks and developing ground-level knowledge. Therefore, contrary to the high-level research-centric view, the willingness and ability of users to undertake a venturesome part plays a critical role in determining the ultimate value of innovations. The venturesomeness of customers also encourages innovators to optimize their offerings for customers' needs and to invest in marketing to them.

NOTES

1. Bhidé, Amar. 1983. "Beyond Keynes: Demand Side Economics." *Harvard Business Review* 61, no. 4 (July–August): 100–110.

2. Mokyr, Joel. 1990. *The Lever of Riches: Technological Creativity and Economic Progress.* New York: Oxford University Press.

3. Rosenberg, Nathan, and L. E. Birdzell Jr. 1986. *How the West Grew Rich: The Economic Transformation of the Industrial World.* New York: Basic Books.

4. Cohen, W. M., and D. A. Levinthal. 1989. "Innovation and Learning: The Two Faces of R&D." *Economic Journal*, September, pp. 369–96.

5. Smith, Adam. 1776. *An Inquiry into the Nature and Causes of the Wealth of Nations.* Modern Library edition. New York: Random House, 1937.

6. Rosenberg, Nathan. 1976. *Perspectives on Technology*. New York: Cambridge University Press.

7. _____. 1982. "Learning by Using." In *Inside the Black Box: Technology and Economics*. New York: Cambridge University Press.

8. Roberts, E. 2004. "Here Be Dragons: The Economics of Enterprise Software Systems." Letter to Members of the Faculty Senate, Stanford University, May 27.

9. Eisenberg, A. "The Door Key That Can't Be Misplaced," *New York Times*, June 10, 2007.

10. Bresnahan, Timothy F., and Shane Greenstein. 1996. "Technical Progress and Co-invention in Computing and the Use of Computers." *Brookings Papers on Economic Activity: Microeconomics* 1996:1–78.

11. Somers, T. M., and K. Nelson. 2001. "The Impact of Critical Success Factors across the Stages of Enterprise Resource Planning Implementations." *Proceedings of the 34th Hawaii International Conference on System Sciences (HICSS-3)*, Maui, Hawaii, January 3–6. CD-ROM.

12. Holland, C. P., and B. Light. 1999. "A Critical Success Factors Model for ERP Implementation." *IEEE Software* May–June , 30–35.

13. Plant, R., and Leslie P. Willcocks. "Critical Success Factors in Internation ERP Implementations: A Case Research Approach." London School of Economics and Political Science Working Paper, May, 2006.

14. Scaffidi, Chris, M. Shaw, and B. Myers. "Estimating the Numbers of End Users and End User Programmers." Proceedings of the 2005 IEEE Symposium on Visual Languages and Human-Centric Computing. FL?HCC'05. 1–8. http://ieeexplore.ieee.org/Xplore/login.jsp?url+/iel5/10093/32326/01509505.pdf?arnumber+1509505.

15. Arora, Ashish, Chris Forman, and Jiwoong Yoon. N.d. "Software," in *Innovation in Global Industries: U.S. Firms Competing in a New World*, ed. Jeffrey Macher and David C. Mower. Washington, DC: National Academies Press.

INNOVATORS AT WORK

A Conversation with Brian Eno

Brian Eno *is a musician, producer, artist, writer, and technologist whose ideas have had an astonishingly wide impact on our culture since the early 1970s. His solo and collaborative records with artists like David Byrne and John Cale have helped inaugurate new genres of music, including ambient generative music, as well as pioneering techniques that became essential to modern sampling. As a producer, he has a long track record of creating essential new sounds with some of the most famous musicians in the world: David Bowie, the Talking Heads, U2, and Coldplay. His art installations have been showcased at locations around the world, and he has even collaborated with the game designer Will Wright to create the generative soundtrack for the game Spore.*

SJ: I'm looking at this card deck of "Oblique Strategies" that you created with Peter Schmidt many years ago, and the little introduction to the set says the cards arose out of "observations of the principles underlying what we were doing." So I guess that's where I want to start: you've had this extraordinarily innovative career in multiple fields. Do you see some underlying principles behind the way you have come upon new ideas?

BE: Anyone who's had children will know that the urge to create—to make something from nothing—is innate. You can't stop kids from doing it: they're perpetually inventing. Sometimes we manage, through our education systems, to multiply that energy: often we manage to stifle it. The trick for me isn't about showing people how to be creative as though they've never been like that before, but rather trying to find ways of recontacting the natural playfulness and curiosity that most people were born with. There are quite a few facets to this, but a very big part of it involves moving away from the idea that "creativity" is an exclusively individual thing, that it springs up in certain gifted individuals, entirely from their imaginations. The more you look at the history of art and science, the more you notice that it is as much to do with the contingencies of the time: the technologies that were around, the conversations that were taking place and so on. This isn't to say that there are no differences between minds, but rather that those differences might be of another order than pure "processing power": they might have a lot to do with the sheer luck of where you happened to be born, of who said what and when, of what tools were available to you.

I think one thing that we don't normally acknowledge is the power of our tools and technologies. We like to imagine that ideas pop fully formed out of our minds as the result of our internal creative processes. And we imagine that we then create the technologies we use in order to realize those creative flashes: so, classically, a scientist has a theory and devises an experimental apparatus to test it. Although this does sometimes happen I think more often it's the reverse that takes place: that it's the technology that precedes the understanding of the principles. This happens in science a lot: a tool is invented, and the tool then leads to some new realization, something that you could now do or see or understand that you could never have understood before. I think that very often happens in the arts. My favorite example—

because it's the one I've spent my life working with—is the recording studio. The multitrack studio was invented for completely mundane reasons so that engineers could more easily balance the vocalist against the rest of the performers. They didn't have to make those critical decisions before the recording; they could do it afterward. But of course, that humble invention gave rise to a whole different way of making music, really a completely different understanding of music.

So in my particular case, a lot of my creative behavior has come from looking at technologies, new tools, and thinking, "You know what, this allows you to do something that nobody ever thought to do before."

SJ: Is there a process for that? How do you explore a new piece of technology?

BE: I spend a fair amount of my time just fiddling around listening for something new. I'm always fascinated when I hear something I haven't heard before, and think, "Wow, nobody's ever done that before." And sometimes I think, "Nobody's ever done that before—but it's fantastic! If I don't get it out quickly, somebody else is going to discover it very shortly." [Laughs] So my process—you could call it noodling, really. It's just playing with the materials, trying to understand where we are now that we weren't yesterday. That's how the idea for Discreet Music came about. It was a very simple discovery that if you connected together two tape recorders in a particular way you could create a very long delay, so that the echo of something comes back five or six seconds after you've played it, then you can play on top of it;

and then you can play on top of the two of them, and the three of them. So you can build up dense layers of material in real time: one person becomes an orchestra. But you could never do that before; the possibility arises entirely out of the technology of tape recorders.

In fact, the funny thing about Discreet Music is that I first did it with *three* recorders, and it took me months to realize that I only needed two! I don't know why but I had these three recorders in a row, and I had two playbacks and one record, and that's how I used it for a long time. And it was at least months, possibly years, before I realized, "You know what, I don't need that third recorder." [Laughs] It was very funny—it had been like magic the first time I did it, so I never questioned the format.

SJ: One other interesting thing about your career is that you've had such a big influence as a producer, in a sense coaxing new musical ideas out of other people. What strategies have you developed in that kind of context?

BE: First of all, the very fact of having somebody who *isn't in the band* and who is suggesting new ways of working is in itself very powerful. Because that person is not part of the political/ diplomatic situation within the band itself. You know, any band that's been together for a very long time has done it partly by being polite to one another; a certain level of decent human rapport. So it's very difficult within a band if somebody does something and you don't think it's a very good idea—it's still quite hard to say, "Look, that's no good. Let's not bother with that." You're duty bound to go through the process of exploring it until the person himself says, "Yeah, it's not that good is it?" Whereas having somebody from the outside coming and looking at a piece without any particular loyalties or prejudices, and saying, "Well, that's working, but I don't think this is working. And this bit over here could work. . . ." People are much more ready to accept an assessment like that from somebody that they know is not personally engaged in the work. So the producer as outsider just in itself is important.

Also, the fact of having to present things to somebody, which is what a band is doing when they're talking to a producer, means that they have to articulate and package the thing, if you like—they have to bring it to some kind of position where somebody else can look at it. It has to be more than a vague idea. So I think it encourages the band to focus on what they're doing. For instance, if I work with someone and I say that I'll be in next Monday and maybe we can have a look at these pieces then. And just doing that makes the band say: "Okay, we've got about fourteen guitars on that one; we should really sort out which ones we want to use before Brian comes along to hear it." So the producer can be the person who catalyzes certain conclusions along the way, who says, "Okay, where is this thing at now—how does it really stand at the moment?"

SJ: We've talked before about your technique of having the members of the band play one another's instruments in the studio. I love that idea.

BE: One of the other things that a producer can do is to think of ways to get people out of their habits. Any group of people who has worked together for a long period of time tends to fall into habits about how things are done. One person always tends to be the person who leads the process; another is the one who supports the leader; another, the one who comes in late and who doesn't say much until the very end; and another one is the stubborn one, counterbalancing the enthusiastic one. And that's all fine—that's part of the chemistry of a group of people working together. But it gets very habitual and it gets quite boring, so I think of ways of upsetting that, turning it into a game actually. So saying today, "You are going to give all the orders; and you, the person who normally does all the talking, you're going to just do what you're told. And you are going to play this instrument that you normally don't ever touch, and in fact that you can't play." [Laughs] So sometimes that does actually yield an immediately usable result. But what does very often happen is that it loosens people up. And it enlarges the envelope of possibilities within which they navigate. I mean, if you tell somebody else to play drums, you have a very simple drumbeat normally, because the person who has taken over the drums isn't the drummer, and, therefore, you start writing and thinking in a different way. It just immediately takes you out of the normal course you would have followed.

SJ: I would think that recording in different cities, which you've often done, would be helpful in the same way—you're deliberately disorienting yourself with some new culture. I mean, I sometimes hear about people recording a record in some exotic place, and I think, "Why are they traveling all the way there when they can just record it at home?"

BE: I think one of the other reasons is simply that: getting away from home. So you're not engaged with picking up the laundry and doing all the normal things for your everyday life. There's nothing else to do except what you're there to do. And I think that really helps a lot. It's the strongest reason for going someplace else. The location is almost irrelevant. What's more relevant is the fact that it's not your normal location.

SJ: As you look over your career, are there periods where you see an unusual cluster of new ideas, where you just feel like you're on some kind of streak? And then are there fallow periods where nothing is really working?

BE: I think there are periods that, when you're in them, seem desperately unfruitful, and you think, "Why am I doing this? I'm completely useless, and I've lost it all." Then an idea finally strikes you, and you suddenly realize that you've been working on it for quite a long time but you weren't aware of it. You've assembled all of the mental and physical tools you need to handle it in what seemed like a fallow period. So I don't really believe in fallow periods anymore. I just think there are periods when you're aware that things are happening, and then other periods where things are happening but you're just not aware of them. There's a lot of time when I just don't know what I'm doing. I was talking to Laurie Anderson the other day; she's on tour and she phoned me and I said, "Do you sometimes wonder why we're all still doing this?" When I look back over my life and think about the times when I felt absolutely confident about what I was doing—it's probably about twenty periods of fifteen minutes or a half hour each, where I suddenly thought, "I know exactly what I'm doing now. I know what this is for; I know what I've been doing; I know what I'm about to do." It's a fantastic feeling and it gives you the energy to keep going for a very long time—because it only lasts a few minutes, before all the—not difficulties really—the *ambiguities* of the situation become evident.

A Conversation with Beth Noveck

Beth Noveck *is one of the most important thinkers—and practitioners—of the new "open government" movement. While directing the Institute for Information Law and Policy at the New York Law School, Noveck created the Peer-to-Patent community patent review project in collaboration with the U.S. Patent Office. The author of the book* Wiki Government, *she served as the United States Deputy Chief Technology Officer from 2009 to 2010, and led President Obama's Open Government Initiative.*

SJ: It seems to me that one consistent theme through everything you've been involved with is the idea of widening the pool of potential experts, recognizing that there are gradients of expertise out there in a much larger part of the population. If government can engage some of that intelligence, we're going to come up with more innovative solutions to the problems that we face. You've been a champion of the phrase open government to describe this movement, but there has been confusion about openness versus transparency, right?

BN: You're exactly right that the notion of innovation is about generating new ideas faster through more interaction with new people and new ideas and creating new conversations. The question is how do you create the mechanisms for that richer and more diverse interchange of ideas so that you can get better ideas into government and solve problems faster. In the current political debates about budget cutting, I pull my hair out because to me the question is not how do I cut a particular service, but how do I deliver that same service using less money and innovative techniques to do the same thing for people that we did before. That's the idea of creating an open government in the sense of open innovation.

If we talk about open innovation as the practices that many firms have adopted, [we're talking about] being more collaborative, where it's companies who are consulting their customers about what designs they should offer in their fall line or it's companies who are talking to their employees about better ideas about how to do the work of the company more effectively, or talking to their suppliers about how they can be more efficient in what they do. A lot of companies are really beginning to get on board with this notion that we have to talk to everyone in the supply chain, if you will, including the suppliers, including the customers, including our employees. We think about not trying to do everything for ourselves, but instead, set up a network so that we can realize economies of scale.

So it's this notion that we have the tools that allow us to be more collaborative and thereby act according to highest and best use. In the public sector, similarly, the question is how do we leverage, how do we collaborate better, across organizations of government, whether it's federal, state, or local, across entities within government, and between government and the public, to solve problems better by being more collaborative. Now, there's many different visions of ways of making government work better. One of which is "open government" in the sense of "transparent," meaning if we make the workings of government more visible to people, government will become more accountable and work better. My own feeling is [that] that by itself does not produce innovation. We have in this country a very open government relative to a lot of other countries, and increasingly now we do things like publish records of who comes and goes to the White House. Ten Downing Street publishes the salaries, as does the White House, of the people who work there. That does very little in my view to actually change the way that government works. It's very important, I think, not to be confused between transparency for its own sake and collaboration. Open government starts with the focus on how do I create greater collaboration between people rather than simply transparency for its own sake.

SJ: What are some of the mechanisms for that collaboration that you've been most excited about?

BN: I got into doing this work because of an experiment that I ran several years ago. Back in 2005, I posited the idea of what would happen if we actually tried to connect the patent office to an open network of volunteers who would help the patent office in making the decision about which invention deserves a twenty-year grant on monopoly rights. This is not the idea of crowd-sourcing the decision—it was again trying to preserve that independence and public mindedness of the bureaucrat by letting the patent examiner make the judgment. Instead, the idea was to crowd-source the knowledge gathering, the information that informs the decision, knowing that the examiner in Washington, with only a few hours in which to do the job of examining a patent, can't possibly have access to all the relevant info from his or her desk to decide whether the latest component of your cell phone is actually new and original and deserves a patent, or whether the latest drug that's been invented to cure cancer is actually going to, is actually a sufficient enough advance over what came before to deserve that very powerful twenty-year set of economic rights that you get. And so at that point, we didn't have Facebook, we didn't have Twitter. So we had to build the platform that would enable people to volunteer to contribute information to help the patent office, and we had to design a system that would respond to the incentives of the different actors involved. In other words, it wasn't enough to simply say, "Let's throw open the floodgates to any suggestion that anybody wants to give." We have to create a very structured system and then we have to use rating and ranking technologies, something that's very prevalent today, where people rate and rank on Amazon and other sites. That pilot continues to be ongoing with the USPTO [the United States Patent and Trademark Office], it's been launched now in Australia and Japan, and is going to be launched in the UK as this notion of crowd-sourcing expertise becomes more accepted and prevalent. So this was kind of the first experiment of its kind, and it's now something that's in widespread use across government in many ways and in many countries.

The National Archives, for instance, now has a citizen archivist project where they're actually getting help from citizens and tagging old records and going through old records because there's so many more things to go through than their librarians can possibly do alone. I can go on and on and on with examples now, especially now that the technology is so prevalent that the policy is there, the political will is there, increasingly around the world, not just in the United States, to try some of this work. And the tools exist to do this much, much better.

SJ: One of the things I really like about what you're saying is that you're not eliminating that individual judgment. You're not saying individuals and official experts still don't make assessments of things; it's just that those individuals are much smarter if they're connected to a broader network of people, and if they have a broader and more diverse range of inputs to draw upon in making their decisions.

BN: That's the interesting thing about the kind of hybrid of bureaucracy and network, or hybrid of institution and network that I think is the really interesting form that we have yet to fully evolve. Because there are really good things about bureaucracy. The word *bureaucracy* obviously has a really bad connotation. But there are things that are good about this notion of independent, public-minded decision making that is not subject to the influence or capture of market forces or of the political popular will of the moment. So the notion that we have a state that is intended not to veer wildly from one direction to the other with changes within the administration—we have a very small political layer, and then we have this kind of ongoing, four million people whose job it is to keep the ship of state running, regardless of who sits in the Oval Office and to ensure that we don't have these wild swings. Otherwise, we would be Libya. It's one of the great inventions of American culture: the bureaucracy is one of the things we've done best, ironically. It's the stability of the state, and having this regularized procedure and this notion of public-mindedness. One of the things I loved about my time in government [was] the people in the civil service who I met who are inspiring, truly public servants. The stereotype of the bureaucrat, somebody who shows up at 9:01 and leaves at 4:59 and is clocking a paycheck—I didn't meet those people. These are people who are smart people, who do what they do because they care deeply, and they want to do what's right and they believe in their mission of independence and public service. And so the combination of that set of values with the kind of rapid idea generation, creativity, and innovation that the network brings, put together, is a pretty powerful thing. But we don't have the custom yet with how to ask questions or how to answer them across that divide. So that's [what] the interesting, I think, experiments and work of the next couple of years looks like.

SJ: I'm also really interested in something else you've written about and worked on: prizes. A prize-backed challenge is a structure whereby the state creates alternate markets for innovation where the market refuses to incentivize people to generate something on their own. So you create this artificial market where the government or some other institution says: If you solve this problem that serves some social good, that the market isn't solving on its own, you'll make $10 million or you'll make a million, and even in some of the software challenges we've seen, all you need is $10,000 in prize money. You don't need that much money.

BN: You only need free T-shirts!

SJ: But I think that's a pretty interesting space right now.

BN: What I love about the prize-backed challenge as a way of working is, first of all, it helps people on the institutional side frame a question. When you talk about things in terms of a challenge, particularly a challenge backed by a prize, it creates a certain discipline that gets those with the knowledge of what the public interest is and what the social imperatives are—call those the government people, although I think people on both sides of the divide have suggestions about what the suggestions should be. But it gets the public servants to frame the question in a way that people know how to help and how to respond. The big problem right now is, there's lots of people right now who say, "I would love to be involved in and do public service. I would love to be involved in the life of my democracy. I'll gladly do something." But they have no idea what to do. During election season, I know what to do. I know about getting out the vote, I know what that means. I may know what it means to sweep up my local park, or do some kind of local volunteerism, but you tell me, be involved in policy making? What am I supposed to do?

SJ: By the way, one of the reasons why I think all this networked collaboration worked first in elections is that elections have built-in game mechanics. So people always know there's a scoreboard—

BN: There's a winner!

SJ: There's a winner and a loser and I know how to play games. So here, if I do this, I can see this number go up and I'm getting better and I get new privileges. It's as if there's this giant video game that's built into that environment and we have technologies and we have usage patterns that allow people to lock into that. But we don't have them built into civic participation in the same way, once the election is over.

BN: And that's why there is some really interesting thinking being done increasingly on the question of game-ification and you're hearing people like Jesse Schell and others who talk about, wow, if we actually turned it into a game that could get [me] tax credits for turning down my heat, how cool would that be? Jane McGonigal has talked about this: within a game, I know what I'm supposed to do—it's as simple as that. And what prize-backed challenges do partly is this: they tell me what to do. The other thing that's really exciting about challenges is that I think it creates this kind of wonderful, flourishing ecosystem of innovation around a particular problem. What I like is that in some cases, it responds to a market failure by offering a prize to compensate for a lack of funding within the private sector. But in many cases, what it also does is [it] just generates attention and eyeballs and demand around something, and actually allows people to create ideas that then become successful businesses.

SJ: You've seen a lot of projects up close from your work inside the Obama administration and in other capacities. What's one of your favorite examples of open government at work?

BN: One favorite project that I have is the *Federal Register 2.0* project. The federal government publishes the *Register* every day.

It's one of the great innovations of our democracy, above all other countries in the world: the fact that we have a daily gazette, a daily newspaper for our government, in which we put out, every day, all the news about grants that are available and regulations that are pending, actions that are taken by the president.

SJ: I'm not sure I knew that's what the *Federal Register* was! I've heard about it a million times, but I don't think I fully realized exactly what it was until now.

BN: You don't know what it is because it's never been something that the average person would read because it's so densely written in legal jargon; graphically, it's an interface culture we live in and it's very hard to read a document that's intensely small print; it's very hard to look at. So companies hire lobbyists and lawyers who read the *Federal Register* for them and tell them that there's something they should be aware of. So there's a lot of middlemen that make their money in tracking the *Federal Register*. Journalists also read the *Federal Register* to find out what's going on in government. So we have this practice that's existed for seventy-five years, since Roosevelt, of publishing this daily newspaper—we put the information out but you have to get people to read it for you. It's as if we were publishing it in another language known as legalese.

But then a few years ago, in response to a prize-backed challenge to do something with a government data set, three guys sitting in a coffee shop in San Francisco went on data.gov and looked for the biggest data set they could find. And that was ten years' worth of *Federal Register*s in a raw, downloadable format by the National Archives. They said, "We've never heard of the *Federal Register;* we've never looked at it, but man, is this hard to read. We could make this look better." Long story short, they enter their prototype in the competition; they don't get first prize, they get second prize, but the National Archives and government printing office that publish the *Federal Register* noticed and saw their entry and thought, *Wow, that's pretty good.* And they called up the three guys in the coffee shop and they said, "How would you like to remake the *Federal Register* for us?" So three guys, never done business with the federal government before, know nothing about government—they're three citizen coders—they get the job, and within three months, in the rotunda of the National Archives before the Constitution and Declaration of Independence, the new *Register 2.0* is announced by the archivist of the United States, with a copy of the Magna Carta in the background. I mean, the Founding Fathers might as well have been in the room, and these three guys who had to buy a suit for the occasion unveil the new *Federal Register.* If you go look at it at federalregister.gov, it's beautiful. It has pictures, it's searchable, if you want to find out what's new today in your home state. Now, it's still written by government bureaucrats in a language that's not yet as accessible as it should be, but the fact that it's now published in a form that people can read is, I think, if you go and look two years from now, I would bet you the language will be easier to read, because people are now writing it for a new, wider audience. The short of it is, making transparent a government data set, reaching out to citizens with a prize-backed challenge, to do something with that data, is enabling citizens to play a role in making their government work better, make it more effective, and efficient. These are people who you would not have thought of as experts in the *Federal Register*, but what they knew something about was good interface design, how to use technology to solve a problem in a way that folks within the government never would have thought of for themselves. So now we have an innovation that has made the government work better for all Americans.

And the story gets even better—they took the code of their project and made it freely available as an open-source project. And now other people can take it, and in fact I know of other people who are working on the platform, a totally different set of people, who are seeing if they can adapt it so that any city that wants to create its own newspaper can now use that code to be transparent [and] to publicize opportunities for people in the municipality.

These three guys still, at the moment, have day jobs, but it's very likely that what will happen as a result of [their] work is that they will be able to start their own business. So there will be another happy ending to this story, which is generating entrepreneurship, creating new jobs and economic growth. So I love the story because it's very high-minded, involving the National Archives and the Declaration of Independence and three guys sitting in a coffee shop who end up making government work better for all Americans.

A Conversation with Jon Schnur

*As the cofounder and chairman of New Leaders for New Schools, and an important contributor to the education policy of both the Clinton and Obama administrations, **Jon Schnur** has been actively involved in reinventing the American education system for almost two decades. His work has focused on teacher and school leadership quality, charter schools, and reforming urban school systems. He helped create the Race to the Top program, which was introduced as part of the 2009 stimulus package, and is now widely considered one of the most successful innovations in education policy in recent years.*

SJ: I think we all agree that something has started to change in the education space over the past five years or so, in that there's a new interest in innovation in how schools work: how we teach teachers, how we compensate them, how the classrooms are structured. People seemed open to new ideas—why is this happening now?

JS: I started working on this full-time in 1993, and it felt like those of us who were working on education did not have that sense of national focus and urgency and possibility then. And that has changed. I think there are a few drivers. I think one of them is the economic shift; the country's understanding of the role that education plays in tomorrow's economy. It's gotten both educators but also business leaders and the media interested in education. In the 1970s, a quarter of jobs required postsecondary education, and today more than two-thirds require it. In a few decades, to have that kind of macroeconomic shift, it's seismic. People recognize that education is really the key to economic competitiveness, so that's driven people across the political spectrum and the labor business world.

The second thing is that one of the great successes over the past ten or fifteen years is that we in this country now have hundreds of schools serving low-income kids that are getting dramatic results, which is really dispelling the myth that poverty and social background [are] the driver of educational outcomes. When you have really quality schools and quality teaching, they can be a powerful strategy in countering poverty, though of course it's not the only thing that's needed. So we have these proof points of schools that work—some in the better-branded charter schools, but some in traditional public schools, too.

And the third thing that I would say—and this is something that comes out of our work at New Leaders—we started looking in 2004–2005 at schools that were getting really dramatic results compared to schools that were getting only average results. Our team visited a hundred schools and we looked at what patterns were leading to breakthrough improvements in those schools— and the patterns were so consistent. It wasn't just that there was this amazing, charismatic leader who could somehow defy gravity. It was that there were some consistent patterns in different neighborhoods all around the country that actually were pretty similar. So it's not just that individual schools can generate success, but the patterns that drive that success are so consistent that it gives you a sense of confidence that we actually can take this to [a] greater scale.

SJ: Let's talk about the innovation in education that you've been most closely associated with: Race to the Top.

JS: Race to the Top is one vehicle in education to try to support taking some of these breakthrough successes we've seen and help take them to greater scale. During the transition period after the 2008 election, President-elect Obama set aside almost a seventh of the stimulus package for education, and what he proposed was a large amount of funding to prevent layoffs of teachers—in return for significant reform and innovation in the schools. The piece that became the center of the reform and innovation component was Race to the Top. It was essentially a $5 billion carve-out that became a competition. There were three components, but [the] main competition involved $4 billion. Essentially, Obama said to the state governors and state superintendents: "If you agree on significant reform and innovation, if you really focus on continuous improvement in your schools—if you really come up with a plan to do this, we'll give you a share of four billion dollars in this competitive process." Actually, this competitive funding is a small share of education funding nationally— it's $4 billion out of more than $400 billion being spent on education.

SJ: What's appealing about the structure of it is that you have essentially this mix of top down and bottom up: you have the federal government saying here are some macro goals that we think are important, but the specific changes and new ideas and innovation that are going to be most helpful in achieving those goals—we're not going to tell you what those are. That's a very powerful mix.

JS: And it was controversial! When the president proposed this, most of the Republicans opposed it because they didn't want to increase education funds. Many of the Democrats opposed it because they didn't want to fund competition. They just wanted to put the money into existing programs. So there was no constituency for it. And the only reason it got done, I would say, is because the president said, "This is a top priority for me, and in order for me to support this package, I want this to be included." There's no other way this would have happened. There were a few individual members of Congress that were intrigued by the idea, but at the time, it just ran counter to the way both parties were working.

SJ: Are there good metrics on how well it worked?

JS: I think a lot of people would say Race to the Top has been a great success so far, but in another way, I think it's still too early to tell. The successes are—for one, there has been great focus and energy around reform and innovation in education, which has been pushed further by this; and two, I think people cite a lot of the policy changes that states have made, saying that this has been the biggest example of the federal government incent[iviz]ing and driving change in policy. So there are states that had barriers to innovation that have been removed: things like caps on the number of high-quality charter schools, or prohibitions on looking at results-oriented evaluations for teachers and principals. It's interesting—and this is really connected to innovation—a number of states have adopted this "common core" of assessments. Which may not seem like it's related to innovation, but it's actually crucial to innovation, because one problem in the country is that we have all these different bars for success . . . many of them fairly dumbed down. So creating a much higher bar for student success, that's also streamlined, so we have fewer, higher standards for student success across the country—that actually creates a kind of space for innovation nationally. If people can figure out ways to help kids do well on those, they can now have their tools and their ideas spread across the whole country the way you couldn't before.

So I think when you look at it that way, I think you could see Race to the Top as a big success. But, my view is that the proof in the pudding is actually in what happens in schools and school systems and student learning. So in a sense, we've created an opportunity, but the question is do we seize or squander that opportunity over the next three to five years in leveraging those policy changes to drive really dramatic improvements in the way kids learn and teachers teach.

In a sense it's the opposite of No Child Left Behind—instead of mandating something to the entire country, let's empower leaders around the country to figure what they're going to do. And now there are twelve states that have won grant money from Race to the Top—and, you know, there are going to be failures. That's one thing that government has a hard time doing: accepting that there will be failures, and systems that don't succeed. But there are also going to be huge successes, and those successes are going to happen because there wasn't a one-size-fits-all approach that was mandated.

SJ: I'm also interested in the idea itself, and how it came about—it's been attributed to you in many media accounts, but I imagine it's a more complex story than that.

JS: People love to identify one person as the leader or inventor, but in my experience, that's just not the case. With Race to the Top, it was really the product of years of work by a lot of different people. My own perspective was grounded in schools that had breakthrough achievements, and we came up with some very consistent patterns in terms of what was driving those improvements. And again, we didn't train our leaders to do these things; the best leaders just came up with them on their own. It was just that no one had gone around to look at what all these school leaders were doing around the country. So we created this Urban Excellence Framework, but all it was, was this distillation of the patterns that were created by hundreds of leaders and thousands of educators and tens of thousands of students around the country. We just tried to codify that—it's an example of how I was advising President Obama during the campaign, trying to translate everything effective educators and leaders had taught us into policy recommendations.

And then once Arne Duncan was appointed secretary of education, we had a very short time to make a recommendation of what to do on the stimulus and so at that point I was able to work with Arne to put together a memo that was seizing the opportunity of the stimulus to use it as a vehicle for a lot of these ideas. But all that was, was a channel to communicate what people around the country had already been working on.

SJ: What's on the horizon in terms of educational tools that you are really excited about?

JS: One thing I'm really excited about is this process for the common core of assessments that are going to track what it really takes to be able to succeed in college and in a career, and not just fill in the bubbles on some multiple-choice test. Those will be in place, if states choose to adopt them, by 2014, and I think that streamlined higher level of expectation will be enormously helpful.

SJ: It's a bit like the innovation power that you see in technologies when you have a standardized platform. On the one level, you look at it and you say, "Well, the platform just got more boring because it's standardized"; but on the other hand, it allows other people to build on top of it in reliable ways because the platform is defined.

JS: Exactly—and then you'll have healthy competition for who can develop the best curricula. Who can develop the best model? So that's one.

But then there's also something that is more small scale now, but that I think is going to develop into something much bigger in the long run. There are very new innovations that are essentially personalized learning, that give individual kids what they need through a blend of very new technology, with a reinvented teaching role, which creates a new kind of school. People will debate whether it's over the next five or twenty-five years that this becomes much more pervasive, but I think the future of education is going to be in this blend.

There's a new approach being used by schools like Rocketship in California and School of One in New York. At School of One, they have three classrooms brought together in one nicely designed space to work with kids in sixth, seventh, and eighth-grade math. Instead of three separate classes of say, twenty kids, they actually have a larger number of groups with seven to twelve kids supported by teachers or teacher's aides or sometimes working with computers. Data is collected every day on how every kid is doing through a little exit ticket where the kids complete a five-question quiz that measures how they are doing on what they did that day. The responses are analyzed by people and technology after the kids leave and based on what that analysis finds, each night a new schedule is created to help them with the skills they need the next day. So instead of one teacher saying, "Here's my next unit that I've planned three weeks ago for all thirty kids," lesson plans are designed for small groups of kids who are working on different sets of skills that actually draw on different materials and bring them what they need that day. So it sort of reinvents the classroom. It's far from using technology to replace teachers—it actually empowers teachers to meet the needs of every student. It helps teachers decide: How do I create the right learning environment in my classroom? How do I best deploy the technology?

Now, I don't mean to overstate or oversell this—it's still early. I don't think it solves everything or makes it perfect yet, but I do think it gives you a window into what's possible over time. Certainly it is next to impossible for teachers to meet the needs of each individual student in their classroom in today's environment. This opens up a world of potential—with a blended model, technology can be used to ease the administrative burden we put on teachers and enable them to spend more time on instruction.

A Conversation with Tom Kelley

Tom Kelley *is a professional innovator. As the general manager of IDEO, the global design and development firm, Kelley helped lead the firm through thousands of innovation programs over the last twenty years. According to a 2008 ranking by* Fast Company, *IDEO is the fifth most innovative company in the world. Kelley is also the author of two acclaimed books that explain how to build environments and companies that support the creation of new ideas, and do a better job of bringing those ideas to market:* The Art of Innovation *and* The Ten Faces of Innovation.

SJ: So the interesting thing I think about IDEO is this: Most businesses at least pay lip service to being interested in innovation and some are quite good at it. But with IDEO it is literally your business: your job is to come up with new ideas and new products both for other people and for yourselves. And you guys have been in the space for two decades now. Have you seen something change in the climate over that time, in how people think about innovation?

TK: The big one is that innovation [is] now almost universally perceived as this irrepressible force. When my first book, *The Art of Innovation*, came out, I found myself in situations where I had to *justify* innovation—especially in Europe, I was like, wait, you're kidding, right? And that's completely gone away. Every-

body gets it, that they are competing on a global basis with almost everybody else. It's a hot, flat world. And in that world,
clearly, you have to innovate. And to be honest, if you're in a
high-cost country like the United States or a region like Western
Europe, you've got to be extra innovative—because you have to
compensate for the cost differential that you have compared to
some pretty darn competitive and clever places in the world.

SJ: You know, that brief history of the firm reminds me of a question
I've actually thought about a lot—you actually probably have the
best answer to this. The question, really, of design. So much of the
material that I've been writing about is about open networks and
open-source models and big collaborative systems and things like
that. And yet I think there is this sense that people have, that design
is one of those things that doesn't work very well in that context—
that design by committee is a negative phrase for a reason. And yet
you guys have figured out some kind of way to be real innovators in
design, to kind of come up with new, collaborative models at the
same time. Is there a way to design within a larger group that actually works?

TK: I think that a way that we've succeeded in design is to redefine the word. Because, inescapably, when I joined IDEO, design
was about styling. And we didn't start from styling. We were
called at the time David Kelley Design, named for my brother.
But we had no industrial designers; we did zero styling at the
time. Our designers were all engineers; in fact they all had
master's degrees in engineering from Stanford. But I think the
way that the design world, writ large, has succeeded is stretching

it from design, meaning styling, to design thinking, which is to say, a thought process. Back when I was speaking mostly about design, I could see the brains of some business people shutting down. The old definition of design seemed exclusionary. You had to wear a black turtleneck to be a member of that club. But the great thing about design thinking is it's accessible to everyone. It involves mental muscles that some people haven't been using lately, but that everybody has from their childhood.

SJ: And how would you define that kind of thinking, as opposed to other forms?

TK: I am shying away from the use of the words *left* and *right brain*. It involves some humility, this form of thinking, or let's say problem solving, because you don't start with the answer. With the highly trained analytical minds that people are walking around with, you see a problem and you have a reaction. You have an instant answer in some cases. You would say that that answer comes from your expertise, from your informed intuition. And sometimes that answer could be the right one. But the design-thinking approach says: "Of course I see possibilities here. But I want to defer judgment a little bit—I want to take a humanistic approach, I want to first check in with—you know, what do humans do, what do humans need with respect to this problem?"

And then, a part of the design-thinking process is this iterative prototyping. Now, understanding what the human needs are, I think I have some answers, as opposed to *the* answer, and so a good design thinker is really facile, really quick with prototyping, and uses the quickest, cheapest prototyping approach available.

Sometimes that approach doesn't involve going to the machine shop at all. Sometimes it involves storytelling, storyboarding, making a video, whatever, but they get these multiple ideas out on the table, and then they get feedback. In complex problems, they get feedback from all the constituents, and then armed with that, the observation they got from looking at human needs, and then the prototyping, where they learn from each prototype, then they're able to go forward, to pick which thing to implement and then go forward with it. But it starts with that humility—the humility of "I have approaches, but I don't have *the* answer."

So my brother David formed this school at Stanford called the "d school"—the *d* is for *design*. And the concept is that all these great universities in the United States and elsewhere have "B schools"—business schools—and the concept is to try to create something that has the same respectability. So when he went to the president of the university to pitch the idea of the d school, he said: "At Stanford University like at all great universities, we have Nobel-laureate-quality people drilling deeper and deeper into fields of knowledge. Some of those fields are technical knowledge and some are the humanities, but these are brilliant people, working and writing about stuff that lots of people don't even understand because it is so deep and complex." And so David said, "Look, I would like to propose that there might be problems in the world today that are not going to be solved by specialists drilling deeper into their field of knowledge. That there might be problems out there, and it seems like there's kind of a lot of them out there to me, that are going to be solved by going *broader*, by getting a business person in a room with an economist in the room with a scientist in the room with an engineer."

SJ: This is something we've both written quite a bit about, the idea of cross-pollination—trying to make those connections across different fields, or different problem spaces. How do you cultivate that?

TK: The example that pops to mind, and you may know of it, is the Aravind Eye Hospital in India. Dr. Govindappa Venkataswamy comes to America, he visits the McDonald's Hamburger University in the U.S. and gets a view into their operational efficiency, and he says, "I wonder what the McDonald's of health care is." And so this is very far afield from health care by definition. But he's sitting in a fast-food restaurant and he cross-pollinates across national boundaries, across industries, comes up with the Aravind Eye Hospital, and it's an amazing place. I have not been, but I've read a lot about it. They've done something like a million cataract surgeries at an average cost of twenty dollars. And they've got health care outcomes competitive with U.S. companies. So I actually think now there's a second-order opportunity for cross-pollination, which is from Aravind Eye Hospital back to the U.S. health care system. There must be ideas that we could reimport from the Aravind Eye Hospital.

There's a story I've told to a lot of my business audiences about a doc from the emergency room going to watch the pit crew at the Indianapolis 500. He's actually with a group of docs, and they're initially thinking they have nothing to learn from people with grease under their fingernails—but in fact, while they're there they notice that when the guys jump over the wall to service the race cars, they have everything at their fingertips. Each person knows exactly what their job is, and each person has all their tools, all their materials, all their supplies right there at arm's length or in pockets, ready to go. And one of the docs says, "Hey, I work in a business where seconds matter, too, and I don't have that. I see somebody with something major, arterial bleeding, I still gotta send people to get the piece parts, you know, get me three of those and two of those and whatever." So one of the docs said he was going to start pre-kitting stuff right away, that he was going to have on hand, right at his fingertips, some of the things that he was going to need.

So in fact, I would argue with cross-pollination, it's the only way, if you really want to innovate. Because if you think you're going to innovate by reading your industry's trade magazine, good luck with that. Because every other competitor has that trade magazine on their desk. And so it's good for keeping up with your industry, but it's not good for getting ahead of your industry. And so you almost have to be looking elsewhere.

SJ: How do you do that in terms of the internal organization of the company?

TK: Well, one thing is just to make it clear that it's important. So I used to, for years, run some of the management meetings at IDEO. Before that, my brother ran them all. And I would say that the first twenty years of the firm, nearly every group Monday-morning meeting started with show-and-tell. And if you think about it, show-and-tell is very childish, it's very kindergarten-y. But if you think about what show-and-tell is, it's cross-pollination. And so if you have a culture that welcomes that, then you're getting this continuous stimulation of ideas from the outside.

SJ: And what are they showing at show-and-tell?

TK: It's everything. It is a new technology that they've uncovered, it's an interesting book that they've read, it's an event that's going on. If you think of your most precious resource, in any organization, it's attention. The attention of the leaders and the team. Just the fact that you're willing to devote that attention, that kind of precious time, to bring stuff in. Not knowing whether it's going to be good stuff or not. It says it's important.

SJ: One other thing that I think is interesting in the book [*The Art of Innovation*]—you have a whole chapter on brainstorming. And brainstorming, there's been kind of a backlash against it in the last ten years. Is there a legitimacy to that backlash, or are people doing it wrong?

TK: I think those are mostly straw-man arguments. Sure, many brainstorms are being done badly, so they don't get good results. So then let's do them well! At IDEO we get extreme value out of brainstorming. Part of the value comes from tapping into the whole brain of the organization. As a practical matter, on any given project, whether it's an internal project or a project in our case for a client, we may have 550 people at IDEO but you only get like five of those people on your team. So that's a limitation. But, through brainstorming, you can get, for one hour, anybody in the firm. And so I am no longer limited by the content knowledge of my five project team members.

SJ: It sounds like what you're saying is that it's not your normal, everyday team that brainstorms. Instead, the idea is to get new people in, from around the organization—so you get a much more diverse mix of folks for that session.

TK: If in your company, if you walk into the room and you can't tell in thirty seconds, in ten seconds, is this a brainstorm or is this a meeting—then you're not doing brainstorming right, I would argue. In fact, the social ecology of the two are opposites. In a meeting, the boss gets to run the meeting. In a meeting, people take notes; it shows respect for what's going on in the room. In a meeting, if somebody says something stupid, or something that would be a problem, I owe it to my colleagues to say, "Oh, remember, we tried that last year and it failed." So in a brainstorm, all the opposites are true. In the brainstorming, especially in companies where brainstorming is not well entrenched, I gotta ask the boss to leave the room. If people are posturing, if people are waiting for the boss to say something and piling on, that is disrupting the free flow of ideas. The boss should set up the problem if he or she wants to be there, say how important it is, and then leave, so that the ideas can flow. In a brainstorm, I would never want anyone to be taking notes because that withdraws them from the fray. I want them to be right in there. And so, of course, the thing where you share your expertise, your critique, that happens right when the brainstorm is over. But [if] we really critique, it just kills the flow of ideas. So there's an energy to a brainstorming session that makes it unlike a meeting in many, many ways. It's a sprint, not a marathon. You don't—the type of brainstorming we are talking about, you don't do it for eight hours. You don't even do it for the whole afternoon. You do it for sixty or ninety minutes, and then if you've still got more to be done, you bring in another team to work on it, because it's kind of mentally exhausting.

SJ: You have in your Palo Alto offices—there is some amazing, fairly celebrated work space there. How can space be used to encourage this kind of thinking?

TK: Sure, this is a slightly frustrating topic for me because I just feel like there's resistance to the idea. I feel like when I walk around, when I visit corporate America, and I've worked personally with fifteen hundred clients, it's as if somebody decided that space is not important. It's as if they said, "I just want to get everyone on my team a desk, a chair, and a wastebasket because anything more than that, any more attention or effort paid on space, would be wasted, like electricity, or plant watering." It's a utility. We believe the opposite. We believe that space can be strategic, that if you get the space right, it can affect the attitude and performance and behavior of the people on the team. There's a great book out there, it's a coffee-table book, called *I Wish I Worked There*, or something. And it's these great spaces, I think not including IDEO's space, but places like Pixar and Google, and Apple, places like that. And you think, "Wait a minute, so these are the companies that routinely go to the top of the most-innovative-companies-in-the-world list, and they have the most innovative space. Hmm, could that be a coincidence?" You know, I don't think so. It's not like space does the whole thing on its own, but I think that space contributes greatly. And I don't mean beautiful space, I mean, space that has the kind of functional aspects that you want.

Even in Palo Alto, where we're paying some of the highest rents in the world, everybody's got two spaces currently. Everybody's got some personal space and that personal space is shrinking every year, because there's more space being allocated to project spaces. So the practical matter, at IDEO, you spend, as one of the professionals (as opposed to the support staff)—you spend ninety-eight percent of your life in the project world. So that's why we define these project spaces. This is an expensive idea, by the way; the cheaper and more traditional way would be to have conference rooms, so you got your desk and when you meet you go to the conference room. Well, that's a problem, because in a conference room, you gotta generate your energy from scratch every time. So imagine you and I are on a project to change health care in America. And we get together in the conference room, and we've got tremendous energy going on, we've got pictures on the walls of the patients we're thinking about, or the doctors. We've got a diagram of the network of how health care gets paid for in America, and we've got all this stuff—and then the hour's up. We take that stuff down off the walls, our hour's up, we gotta leave the room. Whereas in a project room, all that information stays up for the length of the project. So then you get what's called "persistence of information." As soon as I step back inside of that space, I'm in that project again. That picture of that patient is still up on the wall, and that really complicated network of how the docs interact with the insurance companies is still up there. In fact, it gives me a chance to build on it. Imagine that that complex network gets written on the wall in the conference room, and then it gets erased. Even if you write "Do Not Erase" it gets erased within forty-eight hours.

SJ: I love that because I feel like there is this attitude out there of "yes, we need to be more creative with our space, let's put a foosball table in, and then we're done."

TK: I really do believe that you can tweak the space in ways that make it work. One way that you do that is, you make it a little less sacred. There's a large, successful Fortune 100 company who shall remain nameless, and I spoke at one of their brand-new innovation and learning centers. It was a gorgeous building, and it's only been open like a week, and I went to put up these giant Post-it notes on the walls and they said, "Oh, no, we're not allowed to put anything up on painted surfaces." Come on, you're kidding? If you look at the d school at Stanford—they spent millions of dollars retrofitting this old building there. And you look at it and you think, "Wow, it looks like a kindergarten classroom here." So there's nothing precious in the space at all. Everything's movable, everything's rough-and-ready. And if you've got that going with your space, then everybody feels empowered to make it work for what we're doing today, as opposed to thinking, "Oh gee I have to call somebody in facilities. I'd like to move this from point A to point B, but I'd better not touch it." I think that's a part of space. So I'd be the first one to admit, our space is not always beautiful. It's certainly not cleaned up. It is very messy. But it works.

A Conversation with Katie Salen

Katie Salen *is a pioneer in one of the most innovative hybrid spaces today: the intersection between games and education. The coauthor of* Rules of Play, *a textbook on game design, Salen has been the director of graduate students for the Design and Technology Program at Parsons the New School for Design. She is also the executive director of Institute of Play, which promotes game design in educational environments. She's also actively engaged in bringing these new approaches into real classrooms, as a cocreator of* Quest to Learn, *a public school in Manhattan that bills itself as a "school for digital kids."*

SJ: You are right in the middle of two very interesting innovation spaces right now: the world of education and the world of gaming. Let's start with education: what are the new possibilities for teaching kids that you're most excited about right now?

KS: One of them is a bit of departure from thinking about the classroom as the sole space of learning. For a number of years, there's been a kind of pressure on schools that says the institution itself needed to teach kids everything. And I feel like we're in a moment right now, partially because the digital media stuff allows for connections across space and time, to begin to open up that notion of *where* kids are learning. In the design of the Quest schools, the school is just one part of the learning ecology of the kid. And when we begin to think about experiences that we're designing, we want to think about those experiences as connected . . . they partially take place in the school and are supported by the kinds of structures that schools are pretty good at doing, but they also implicate the after-school space and they implicate the home space. And they tend to be wrapped together by things like a social network site that we designed for the school that allows kids to also have connections to people beyond the walls of their neighborhoods and beyond the walls of their school. So that notion of the connectivity across time and space and people and resources is, I think, something to be hugely excited about.

SJ: That's great. Obviously there's been so much focus on the game principles that the Quest schools are using. How is that working, now that you've got kids actually in classrooms?

KS: What we tried to do is design the school from the ground up around core principles of games. One way that manifests itself is in classes that deal with more than one subject. In a game you would never just encounter math or science on its own; you're actually working on a complex problem that calls in different kinds of knowledge simultaneously. So we have classes with names like The Way Things Work, which is an integrated math and science class. We have one called Codeworlds World, which integrates math and English-language arts. And each of those classes is trying to look at a core method or way of working with knowledge. That's something that games do. The curricula are structured around complex problems that kids are dropped into that last ten to twelve weeks. The problems are really engaging and interesting, but there's no way on day one that students can solve them. So it gives rise in kids to what we call a "need to know." And that's the core thing we care about in terms of curriculum design. Can we create really compelling learning experiences where kids have an interest in learning about fractions or have [an] interest in learning how to write a memoir or persuasive essay because they're working on a problem they think is interesting? That's one way that the game stuff manifests itself: we call them "missions," and the missions get broken down into smaller classes, which are sort of smaller problems that help kids do work on a bigger problem.

In addition, kids design games as part of the curriculum. We have a big focus on systems thinking in the school. We think that's a key twenty-first-century literacy. And we've found that when kids make games . . . that they're a really great tool for understanding how systems work in action. Games are like little super minisystems, and [the kids] can see change over time, and they can understand the core principles of systems thinking. And so we have a yearlong class in game design in sixth grade. Kids learn how to makes games, they learn the language of games, and then they're able to take that language and apply it to systems, which they're then working with in all of their other classes.

SJ: My kids have been playing this game Dawn of Discovery, which is an incredibly cool game. And they've been obsessed recently with building a cathedral in the game. It's amazing all the different kinds of problems you have to solve to get to the point in the game where you can build a cathedral—and all the different kinds of thinking that they have to do. They have to think like a city mayor, they have to think like a merchant, they have to think like a farmer, because of all the different layered objectives. They will claw their way downstairs to be able to play this game to build a medieval cathedral. So to me, the question is: how do you tap that in other environments?

KS: Exactly. One other key part of the Quest schools is that we have a group of game designers that are embedded in the school, and they're there every day, and they work with teachers to codevelop the curriculum. And so we have this little working game-design studio called Mission Lab, and our designers build games for part of the curriculum. They help the teachers come [up] with ideas around these interesting problems to drop kids into, and help develop learning activities. Probably 65 percent of the materials they produce are nondigital. So we have a whole host of paper-based games, and board games and social games that have been designed to help surface types of content and skills that the teachers are interested in working with the kids on. And then there's another part that is digital. We have this mixed-reality lab in the school where we codevelop motion-based games with the teachers. So sometimes when you go to the school, it looks really nondigital. Kids are reading from printed books, and they're working with paper-based games, and they're writing essays by hand. And other times you go there and kids are on iPads and there's a group clustered around laptops and the mixed-reality lab is going. So for us, it's just about finding the right tool for the right problem that the kids are working on. And it's different for different kids. Sometimes we'll design a game that helps support a group of kids that are either really accelerated in their learning, some are in the middle, or they're needing some support around something that they're not understanding. So not all kids are always on the same platform or using the same set of tools.

We do talk about it as a school for digital kids, and all that's intended to signal is that we think there's a set of core competencies that are necessary in the world today. And part of those are around understanding how to navigate the digital. One, just learning how to use the tools, but also, what does it mean to be online? What does it mean to intelligently search for information? It's at your fingertips, but how do you actually find it? That's something that we believe you have to support kids in learning how to do. Two, how do you work in teams, how do you collaborate across time and space with people that aren't literally sitting next to you? We value all of those things, and the curriculum also supports that work. So we talk about the school bridging traditional literacies, like reading and numeracy, writing, but also getting at twenty-first-century skills. And that's where the digital tools become really key.

SJ: That kind of gets to my second big question, which [has to do with] the Quest schools' goal of teaching innovative thinking. How do you create environments that encourage that kind of thinking?

KS: One thing is, we really believe in learning by doing. We talk about learning to *be,* rather than learning *about.* And we actually try to pose questions or problems for kids that don't have singular answers. They're recruited to become creative thinkers, and are challenged to come up with some kind of solution, or some kind of attempt at understanding. And so we have a whole set of competencies in the school around design thinking, including designing innovation, and we have one around designing play. We're really interested in helping kids really take on identities as innovators. We care deeply that they feel like they can come up with ideas to solve problems in the world that matter to them. Even if those problems are fictional problems that they're interested in. We believe that kids can be empowered if they have tools to know that they can make things that can create change in the world.

SJ: What's an example of that?

KS: The kids right now in the seventh grade—The Way Things Work class, which is math and science—they're working on a mission around "change agents." They're collaborating with a group of sustainability engineers in Brooklyn. They've been given a mission around becoming a change agent in the world and understanding what that means. At the start of the mission, they were introduced through video profiles and Twitter feeds to a set of experts that considered themselves change agents. Each of them has a profile showing their skills; all of the profiles are different. There's one person that's a radio producer, another person who was an interactive data-visualization designer, and someone else who was an engineer. Students began to inquire about who these people were, what they needed to know to do their job, and what kind of change they were trying to make in the world. The kids were then charged with working toward a set of what we call "badges." These are made up of clusters of skills that a student can demonstrate competency in. So you might earn a badge as a habitat guru. The students could pledge a badge, which means that they will work to learn the skills that make up that badge, in order to earn it. They do that by researching a problem that the person who has that badge has been working on, to understand what the issue is. And then the students propose a project that they think uses the skills represented in the badge, in a way that creates change in the world. The problem might be that there's too much trash in New York, or doing something around smoking; kids have all kinds of things that they're interested in.

It really puts the students in the position of thinking like designers, and having to recruit all of the knowledge that you need to have as a designer. What does it mean to frame a problem? What does it mean to iterate and propose solutions to something and test it out and get feedback on it? And how do you refine solutions, how do you test them? We actually see tremendous creativity on the part of the kids in the school. We don't yet know if the school attracts kids that have that disposition already or whether there's something really robust about the curriculum that's leading kids into these incredibly creative but also really rigorous kinds of spaces.

SJ: What's your own innovation process in terms of your collaborators and your own thoughts?

KS: What I find is that I tend to be very interested in types of collaboration with people that know stuff that I don't know. Even when I worked on *Rules of Play*, I was less interested in writing a book about game design for game designers to make more games; I was more interested in writing the book for people that weren't game designers—people who could make things that were influenced by the way that games work and the way that players think. So I've always been interested in connecting to people that are in adjacent domains to me. In some ways this work with the schools was a really natural progression from just trying to understand how games work, which was a body of work that I was doing for a while, and the interest I had in the transgressive qualities and transformative qualities in play. I then started to look at teachers as a kind of counterpart citizens to game designers. When you look at the process of what game designers do, it almost mimics, step for step, what great teachers do. Great teachers constantly think about how to engage their students. They're constantly thinking, what's an interesting problem space that I then need to structure, that lets those kids feel like they're owning that space and are learning and doing stuff and celebrating? Once you begin to see that connection in the disciplinary profiles, it just sort of made sense to say, "Well, couldn't we design something that would put all of this together?" And because I'm a designer, I think it's important to make things in the world. There's a lot of really interesting work that I've been a part of with the MacArthur Foundation's Digital Media and Learning initiative— tons of interesting theory and research, that schools have for the most part, traditionally, been really hostile to . . . There's just infrastructures in place that don't allow for this outside work to come in, in ways that make sense.

I never aspired to open a school or work in secondary education. It was more that I felt we needed a demonstration in space for all of this amazing work that people were doing, all of these ideas; it needed to be something that could be co-created with kids and teachers. And so the school itself has become an innovation space for a number of different people. It has been one for me, but also for all of the people that work on my staff, who are reimagining roles for game designers. And it's repositioning the kind of creativity that teachers have but in many cases haven't been allowed to express.

SJ: Do you still meet teachers outside the school who are hostile to these ideas or is there some sense in everyone that the experimentation at least is worthwhile? Or are people still like: "Games? What the hell are you doing?"

KS: I would say that it's [the] more institutional structures that are hostile. And I just mean that in the way that it's oil and water. There's a way that they structurally just don't come together. I would say that in general . . . [with] almost anyone that I've interacted with in an education space, there is at least a possibility, a possibility for something to happen around this work. I think they're quite open to it. Now, there's still a tremendously resilient mental model around games as a waste of time, and nonrigorous, and so that is still there. But all it takes is bringing someone into the school and actually putting them through an experience of what the kids are doing, then they're like, "Oh, okay, I get it." With the mixed-reality labs, Joel Klein, while he was Chancellor . . . he came to visit the school the day after it opened. And I said: "Come into the space, you need to take off your shoes, come on the mat." I started saying, "Here's this problem. What do you want to do? What's your theory about what's going on?" And he got into it. He just understood the learning model in a way that he didn't before. Which is our whole theory of learning by doing. That's been, as you know, a problem with games, this over-the-shoulder critique in journalism. Sure, games actually do look like a waste of time if you're staring at them over the shoulder of a player. If you actually play the game, you realize there's a set of things going on there in terms of what your mind's doing, as well as the social dimension.

SJ: If you're getting the chancellor to take his shoes off, that's already progress!

KS: [Laughing] He was such a good sport about it.

A Conversation with Ray Ozzie

Ray Ozzie *has been one of the most influential innovators in the world of software for three decades now. After graduating from the University of Illinois at Urbana-Champaign in 1979, he worked on important early applications like Visicalc and Lotus Symphony, before setting out on his own to form Isis Associates, where he created the product that eventually became Lotus Notes. Ozzie then founded Groove Networks, which developed powerful collaboration tools before the term "social software" had even been coined. After Groove was acquired by Microsoft, Ozzie eventually took over the role of chief software architect from Bill Gates, where he served until late 2010.*

SJ: Let's start with your own process. If you look back over your career, and think about ideas that you had on your own or in groups, do you see different patterns or processes in the way that you work, or the kind of environments that have been particularly fruitful?

RO: It feels as though it's a very personal thing, in terms of the different people I would classify as innovators. For me, I've got to create white space in some way that maps to my lifestyle, and that has varied based on how old my kids were, what stage my businesses were in. Everybody has to find some way of introducing that space where you can get out of the day-to-day-to-day stuff that we all impose upon ourselves. For me, the consistent patterns are—and I know this is weird—we have a lake house and we have a place on the ocean, so getting out and boating by myself for a few hours, especially when the weather is rough, it helps. I don't know why, but when I'm doing something that's not putting my body into normal reactive patterns—I'm sure athletics would do the same thing—where I'm trying to deal with this wave, or something about the weather, it's freeing up some other part of my mind, and I come up with a bunch of ideas. I have to have a stack of notes while I'm out there.

SJ: That sounds dangerous!

RO: It is dangerous. I'll stop, I'll write some stuff down . . . so that's one kind of randomness. I don't know how many people do it, but while sleeping, those background threads are still running. This happened last night: I wake up at 2:30 A.M., or 3 A.M., and something is rolling around, some problem that I solved or that won't go away. And I have to find some notepad and write stuff down because during the day I'm just not solving it. The other thing is, and I guess this ties in with the boat in a little way, but I do well when I put myself into a disoriented or exhausted situation. International travel is one of best times for me to think differently. When I'm not so much time-zone confused, but when I'm in Asia in particular, and I can't really get around as well, it helps get me out of that normal pattern. And again, that's been a repeatable thing over the years.

SJ: It's the power of disorientation.

RO: Exactly.

SJ: I have this thing where I'm constantly going somewhere to give a speech, for two days or three days, and I'm dropped in a city in Asia or Europe or somewhere like that. And I'll be there for three days. And I'll have one day to just get adjusted. Then I give my speech, and then I have my bonus day. And I have this routine of just walking out and roaming around for three hours more or less without a map. And then finding someplace to have dinner kind of on my own. And then I sit there at dinner by myself with my little notebook. And there's some great ideation process that happens for me at those times— from the cultural disorientation as well as the time zone.

RO: I completely agree. For me, it's similar to that. But I also am fascinated by mass transit. Tokyo is amazing for this. I like looking at people, I like staring at them and wondering what they're doing with their lives. Looking at what they're using to communicate or entertain themselves, and then go from place to place in the city that I might not have been.

I like the word *disorientation* because the whole thing I'm trying to escape is orientation. In fact, this is what I'm doing at this moment in my career right now. For thirteen years, from 1984 till 1997, I worked on this thing that came to be called Lotus Notes. But it started as nothing, at zero, I started a little start-up, and it went up, up, up, and then at 1997, I left IBM and returned to zero. It was just a complete separation. Because I saw this Internet thing going on and I wanted to be part of it. And I knew I couldn't do it from the orientation that I was in. Nineteen ninety-seven happened to be thirteen years ago. I just returned to zero, and I am now disoriented, trying to find a good orientation to latch onto. It's just the way I work.

SJ: How did the idea for Lotus Notes come about?

RO: The Lotus Notes story is one of those situations where I and several other people—the people who ended up being my cofounders—were exposed to a system that we couldn't shake. It became an itch that we needed to scratch. And the thing that we ultimately built, both the ethos and the name itself, came from that thing that we were exposed to. The product we ultimately built was actually a lot different. But the original experience was the common thread between us.

This was in 1974 through 1977, and there was a group of us who were exposed to this Plato system at Urbana-Champaign in Illinois. This was on the early side of computer science; we were still using punch cards in our computer-science classes. But this Plato system was built by this creative eccentric, Don Bitzer, who believed that computers could change education. He didn't know what couldn't be done. He wanted to build graphics terminals with multimedia, audio. He invented the plasma panel, in order to have a graphics terminal. He built an audio device for it. That left an imprint in and of itself. I love being around people who just don't believe things can't be done, or don't know that they can't be done, and just build whatever the concept requires. But on the software side, we were all exposed to things that ultimately we'd get used to in the Internet. It was the emergence of online community. And there was probably a community of ten thousand people, five thousand at Urbana, Illinois, and another five thousand around the world. There were online chats, online discussions, interactive gaming, news. It was a full-fledged community. And there was this thing called Notes that did e-mail, personal notes, and discussions, group notes. And after we left, and went into the real world and got our jobs (they went to DEC, I went to Data General), that was the thread that we kept coming back to. We were like: these are interesting computers, but where are the people? And so basically we would get together weekend after weekend, month after month, year after year, and say: "We have to bring the people back into the equation."

SJ: So what, that's seven years that the memory of the system is in your head before you actually started to build it?

RO: Well, it went kind of like this: '78 was when we left and came east from Illinois. Eighty-one was when I wrote the first business plan for it and tried to begin getting funding. Eighty-three I realized I couldn't get funding, so I did a deal with Mitch Kapor, and '84 was when the deal with Mitch let me spin out and start working on it in earnest.

SJ: So six, seven years. It reminds me so much of something in my own life, although I didn't do anything nearly as epic. I was in college from '86 to '90 and HyperCard came out in '87. I've never really been a programmer, but I lost a whole semester trying to build this

HyperCard application basically for keeping all my notes and research. (Which eventually fed into my interest in applications like
DEVONthink and the commonplace-book tradition.) But the main
thing I got out of HyperCard was that it really prepared me for the
Web, by working in that hypertextual environment. So I dabbled
with HyperCard and then I kind of put that experience away for
seven or eight years—but then in '94, when the Web started to break,
I was just prepared for it. The first time I saw it, I was like: oh, I know
exactly what this is going to be.

RO: That's a reoccurring theme also. You are the sum in many
ways of your experiences and you get these success patterns, failure patterns, sometimes those patterns help—like what you just
described. But sometimes those patterns hurt, because they con-
strain your outlook. Something that might not have worked before might work now, because the environment has changed. But
the innovators that I know that are successful keep testing those
patterns over and over and over because people around them
change and the technology environment changes. And so you
might look at somebody and say: "You're a one-trick pony. You
keep building the same thing over and over." But it's a good
thing! That means you're taking those patterns and just recasting
them continuously against changes in the environment. And if
you believe passionately in a pattern, it's great. Go for it!

I'm selfishly defending this viewpoint, because I am a one-trick
pony. I believe in this social stuff and I'm out there right now trying to figure out how the mobile services world changes the way
that we interact with one another. How has the embrace of this
second life on the Internet changed the way that people will embrace interaction, where they might have rejected it before?

SJ: You used the phrase *background process* before. That strikes me as being really important. In my personal experience, the people I've been around that are good at innovating are able to just keep these background threads alive so that they can bring them to the foreground when they do become relevant. They're focused on one thing, but there are like nine things in the background. You never know when one of those things is going to suddenly jump to the foreground.

RO: Exactly. And just to geek out on computer architecture for one moment, I used to actually think of them as background threads, like threads of execution, but that actually doesn't scale, because you're exposed to many, many things, and you're not going to spin up a new thread every time you've got an idea—you'd run out of capacity. So what I think is going on, and there must be a physiological basis for this, I think it's more synchronous; it's more of a standing query. You have formulated a pattern, and you're looking for this and this within a set of knowns in the pattern. You've got all of these standing queries in your brain. And so when you are exposed to new things, they are new events that are being generated that are mapped against all the standing queries. And then something fires.

SJ: That's exactly what it is. I love that. So let's think about this sort of thing in an organizational context. You've talked about the difference between "emergent" and "directed" innovation.

RO: Sure, it's very simply that emergent is bottom up, like a coral reef that grows different things that mutate. It's basically building up capabilities from the ground up. It's a very inefficient process. It requires lots of failure for some success to pop up—but what pops up in an emergent basis generally takes shapes that people don't expect. Which is really cool. It combines X, Y, and Z in a way that, if you'd actually been thinking about it, you probably wouldn't have approached it because it wouldn't have matched a pattern that you had already had in your mind. And so, within corporate environments, things that really do resemble more basic research, not applied research, not product development, do add some level in intentional serendipity. That is an asset that I did see that I respected within the Microsoft environment. And IBM. It's hard to foster that, and I don't know of a sustainable model, but it's helpful. It's clearly what's happening in the start-up ecosystem right now. I mean you have base technology improvements that are happening, and you've got little tiny tests, that are happening with one, two, three, four people that get angel-funded or not. Anything that can be done, will be done. Interesting tests emerge, or opportunities, from that kind of environment.

When I say directed what I mean is this: You have either an existing, successful approach, or an existing high-value problem that you know you need to solve. You know generally how to solve it. Let's say it's: I have people who need to work together; I need people to work together who are far apart; I have people that need to work together that use documents. You start introducing a few constraints, or a few known models, and try to innovate around the edges, using those core constraints. Or it's something like: We need to go to the moon. We can break that down into ten pieces, each of those submissions, and go ahead and innovate around that constraint. And you can get some amazing stuff. And both of them are tremendously important, but they're both better when combined, I think. I think the directed approach accelerates fleshing out which of the emergent ones are useful, and can be brought forth very quickly. And without the emergent, you keep thinking about things the same way, over and over and over.

SJ: That's one of the questions that I got that kind of surprised me when I was out promoting *Good Ideas*. In fact I still get it when I'm talking about it. Which is, people say, all this stuff is really helpful and interesting for generating ideas and stumbling across new things, but how do you tell when an idea is a good one. And I'm always a little stumped.

RO: I'm just so excited, so enamored with how things have evolved, because of the Internet and because of open source and because of services that now let us get out there with ideas, and test them in public with real people. Historically, a lot of our industries, especially any IP-based industry, grew up with heavy constraints on the distribution chain—broadcast television, print books, shrink-wrapped software, music on vinyl discs. The distribution mechanism defined a lot going all the way back to the creation of the work itself. And again, sometimes that helped because constraints having two sides of an LP with end songs, say—sometimes can actually help shape the medium. Or help shape the content. But it also introduced that massive constraint. So in software, the whole notion of product planning, and research, and all this stuff, was all based on the fact that you knew you could only get something out there once every two or three years, because of the nature of the distribution channels. So you'd better do the best job you can at incorporating what you know from the outside. That's just so different now. It's tremendous.

SJ: I agree, but one of the questions I've always had is how portable are these kinds of innovations and new models of collaboration outside the world of software?

RO: I actually believe that most IP-based product development falls into the same general category of software. If you're building a drug compound, for instance, the same laws should apply. The basic innovation here tends to be that more complex things can be developed by more people who are not in the same place at the same time, which is really neat. For good, bad, and ugly, thanks to the Internet, we're exposed to all these different ways that other people think, and we have lots of capacity to that can be brought together to solve problems—across all industries. So that's a fundamentally transformative thing.

SJ: So it's a great time to be back at zero and trying to get disoriented...

RO: Oh, it is. It sure is.

CREDITS AND PERMISSIONS

ABOUT THE CONTRIBUTORS

A writer, management consultant, and social ecologist, **Peter Drucker** was one of the most influential figures in the field of management theory and practice. Called the "man who invented management" by *BusinessWeek*, Drucker developed one of the country's first executive MBA programs at Claremont Graduate University, where he taught until 2002. He was the author of many books, including *The Daily Drucker* and *The Effective Executive*. Drucker received the Presidential Medal of Freedom, the nation's highest civilian honor, in 2002 and passed away at age ninety-five in 2005.

Stewart Brand is cofounder and president of the Long Now Foundation and cofounder of Global Business Network. He also founded and edited the *Whole Earth Catalog* and has written several books, most recently *Whole Earth Discipline: An Ecopragmatist Manifesto*.

Originally educated and employed as a chemist, **Teresa Amabile** is the Edsel Bryant Ford Professor of Business Administration in the

Entrepreneurial Management Unit at Harvard Business School, where she also serves as Director of Research. Currently teaching Leadership and Organizational Behavior at HBS, Amabile was the host and instructor of Against All Odds: Inside Statistics, a twenty-six-part instructional series originally produced for broadcast on PBS. She is the author of *Creativity in Context* and *The Progress Principle*.

American urban studies theorist **Richard Florida** is a professor and the head of the Martin Prosperity Institute at the University of Toronto's Rotman School of Management. Named one of *Esquire*'s Best and Brightest alongside venerable figures like Bill Clinton and Jeffrey Sachs, Florida heads the private consulting firm Creative Class Group and is senior editor at the *Atlantic*. He was appointed to Business Innovation Factory's Research Advisory Council and was recently named European Ambassador for Creativity and Innovation. He is the bestselling author of *The Great Reset*, *The Rise of the Creative Class*, *Who's Your City*, and many other books.

Clayton Christensen is the leading authority on the theory of disruptive innovation, an innovation that helps create a new market and value network while disrupting the existing network. A four-time recipient of the McKinsey Award by the *Harvard Business Review*, Christensen is the Robert and Jane Cizik Professor of Business Administration at Harvard Business School. He cofounded the management consultancy Innosight and investment firm Rose Parks Advisors in 2007, followed by nonprofit think tank Innosight Institute in 2008. He is the author of *Disrupting Class*, *The Innovator's Prescription*, *The Innovator's Dilemma* and *The Innovator's Solution*.

Eric Von Hippel is a professor of technological innovation in the MIT Sloan School of Management, and a professor in MIT's Engineering Systems Division. He specializes in research related to the nature and economics of distributed and open innovation. He is the author of *Democratizing Innovation* and *The Sources of Innovation*.

Stefan Thomke, an authority on the management of innovation, is the William Barclay Harding Professor of Business Administration at Harvard Business School. He has worked with U.S., European, and Asian firms on product, process, and technology development, organizational design and change, and strategy. He is chair of the Executive Education Program Leading Product Innovation, which helps business leaders in revamping their product development processes for greater competitive advantage, and is faculty chair of HBS executive education in India. Professor Thomke is also on the core faculty of the Advanced Management Program where he teaches the course Leading Innovation. He is the author of the books *Experimentation Matters: Unlocking the Potential of New Technologies for Innovation* and *Managing Product and Service Development*.

John Seely Brown is the former head of Xerox's Palo Alto Research Center and was the chief scientist at Xerox. He is the independent cochairman of the Deloitte Center for the Edge and a visiting scholar at the University of Southern California. He is coauthor of the bestselling book *The Social Life of Information*. He lives in Palo Alto, California.

John Hagel III is the cochairman of the Deloitte Center for the Edge. He is the author of a series of bestselling business books, including *Net Gain*, *Net Worth*, *Out of the Box* and *The Only Sustainable Edge*. An alumnus of McKinsey's Silicon Valley office, he lives in Burlingame, California.

Geoff Mulgan recently became the CEO of the National Endowment for Science Technology and the Arts after acting as chief executive of the Young Foundation, a center for social innovation in the UK. A visiting professor at University College, London, the London School of Economics, and the University of Melbourne, Mulgan was the director of Policy and director of the Prime Minister's Strategy Unit under British Prime Minister Tony Blair. He is an adviser to many governments around the world and the author of several books including *Connexity*, *Good and Bad Power*, and *The Art of Public Strategy*.

With more than twenty years of research behind him, **Amar Bhidé** is a leading authority on innovation and entrepreneurship. The Thomas Schmidheiny Professor at Tufts University's Fletcher School of Law and Diplomacy, Bhidé is a member of the Council on Foreign Relations and a Fellow of the Royal Society of Arts. He previously served as Laurence D. Glaubinger Professor of Business at Columbia University and as a faculty member of Harvard Business School and University of Chicago's Graduate School of Business. He is the author of *A Call for Judgment*, *The Venturesome Economy*, *The Origin and Evolution of New Businesses* and *Of Politics and Economic Reality*.

Steven Johnson is the author of the bestsellers *Where Good Ideas Come From*, *The Invention of Air*, *The Ghost Map*, *Everything Bad Is Good for You*, and *Mind Wide Open*, as well as *Emergence* and *Interface Culture*. He is the founder of a variety of influential websites—most recently, outside.in—and writes for *Time*, *Wired*, the *New York Times*, and the *Wall Street Journal*. He lives in Marin County, California, with his wife and three sons.

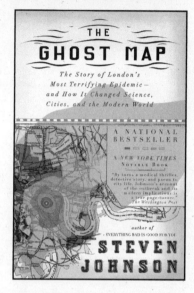
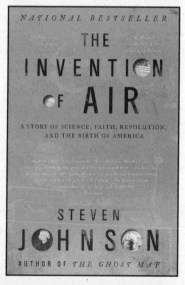
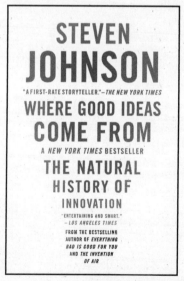